Focus on WRITING 4

John Beaumont

John Beaumont, Series Editor
Borough of Manhattan Community College
City University of New York

ALWAYS LEARNING

PEARSON

Focus on Writing 4

Pearson Education, 10 Bank Street, White Plains, NY 10606

Staff Credits: The people who made up the *Focus on Writing 4* team, representing editorial, production, design, and manufacturing, are Pietro Alongi, Rhea Banker, Danielle Belfiore, Elizabeth Carlson, Nan Clarke, Aerin Csigay, Dave Dickey, Christine Edmonds, Oliva Fernandez, Barry Katzen, Penny Laporte, Jaime Lieber, Tara Maceyak, Amy McCormick, Barbara Perez, Joan Poole, Debbie Sistino, Jane Townsend, and Adina Zoltan.

The Grammar Presentation charts in *Focus on Writing 4* are adapted from *Focus on Grammar 4, Fourth Edition*, by John Beaumont, Pearson Education, White Plains, New York, © 2012.

Cover image: Shutterstock.com
Text composition: ElectraGraphics, Inc.
Text font: New Aster

Library of Congress Cataloging-in-Publication Data
Haugnes, Natasha, 1965–
 Focus on writing. 1 / Natasha Haugnes.
   p. cm.
 Includes index.
 ISBN 0-13-231350-2 — ISBN 0-13-231352-9 — ISBN 0-13-231353-7 — ISBN 0-13-231354-5 — ISBN 0-13-231355-3 1. English language—Textbooks for foreign speakers. 2. English language—Rhetoric—Problems, exercises, etc. 3. Report writing—Problems, exercises, etc. I. Title.
 PE1128.H3934 2011
 428.2—dc22
                                                                                          2011014764

PEARSON LONGMAN ON THE **WEB**

Pearsonlongman.com offers online resources for teachers and students. Access our Companion Websites, our online catalog, and our local offices around the world.

Visit us at **pearsonlongman.com**.

Printed in the United States of America
ISBN 10: 0-13-231354-5
ISBN 13: 978-0-13-231354-4

4 5 6 7 8 9 10—V082—16 15 14 13

Contents

To the Teacher

Focus on Writing is a five-level series that prepares students for academic coursework. Each book in the series gives students an essential set of tools to ensure that they master not only the writing process, but also the grammatical structures, lexical knowledge, and rhetorical modes required for academic writing. The series provides an incremental course of instruction that progresses from basic sentences (Book 1) and paragraphs (Books 1–3) to essays (Books 3–5). Grammar presentation and focused grammar practice are correlated to *Focus on Grammar*.

A Process Approach to Writing

Over the past 30 years, the *writing process* approach has become the primary paradigm for teaching writing. As cognitive research shows, writing is a recursive process. When students practice the entire writing process repeatedly with careful guidance, they internalize the essential steps, thereby improving their writing and their confidence in themselves as writers.

Each unit in each book of *Focus on Writing* provides direct instruction, clear examples, and continual practice in the writing process. Students draw on their prior knowledge, set goals, gather information, organize ideas and evidence, and monitor their own writing process. Students write topic-related sentences and use them in a basic paragraph (Book 1); they focus on writing an *introduction*, *body*, and *conclusion* for a paragraph (Books 2–3) or essay (Books 3–5). Whether students are writing a group of related sentences, a paragraph, or an essay, they produce a complete, cohesive piece of writing in *every* unit.

Predictable Step-by-Step Units

Focus on Writing is easy to use. Its predictable and consistent unit format guides students step by step through the writing process.

■ PLANNING FOR WRITING

Students are introduced to the unit theme through an engaging image and high-interest reading. Brainstorming tasks develop critical thinking and serve as a springboard for the unit's writing assignment. Vocabulary building activities and writing tips related to the topic and organizational focus of the unit provide opportunities for students to expand their own writing.

■ STEP 1: PREWRITING

In Book 1, students learn the basics of sentence structure and are encouraged to combine sentences into cohesive paragraphs. They choose between two authentic academic writing assignments, explore their ideas through discussions with classmates, and complete a graphic organizer.

In Books 2–5, students learn the basics of a rhetorical structure (e.g., narration, description, opinion, persuasion, compare-contrast, cause-effect, or problem-solution) and choose between two authentic academic writing assignments. Students explore their ideas through freewriting, share them with classmates, and complete a graphic organizer.

STEP 2: WRITING THE FIRST DRAFT

Explanations, examples, and focused practice help students to prepare for their own writing assignment. Writing tasks guide students through the steps of the writing process as they analyze and develop topic sentences, body sentences, and concluding sentences (Books 1–3) and continue on to draft thesis statements and complete introductions, body paragraphs, and conclusions (Books 3–5). At all levels, students learn how to use transitions and other connecting words to knit the parts of their writing together.

STEP 3: REVISING

Before students revise their drafts, they read and analyze a writing model, complete vocabulary exercises, and review writing tips that they then apply to their own writing. A Revision Checklist tailored to the specific assignment guides students through the revision process.

STEP 4: EDITING

Grammar presentation and practice help students make the connection between grammar and writing. An Editing Checklist ensures students check and proofread their final drafts before giving them to their instructors.

Helpful Writing Tools

Each book in the series provides students with an array of writing tools to help them gain confidence in their writing skills.

- *Tip for Writers* presents a level-specific writing skill to help students with their assignment. The tips include asking *wh-* questions, using conjunctions to connect ideas, identifying audience, using descriptive details, and using pronoun referents.

- *Building Word Knowledge* sections give students explicit instruction in key vocabulary topics, for example, word families, collocations, compound nouns, and phrasal verbs.

- *Graphic organizers* help students generate and organize information for their writing assignment. For example, in Book 1, they fill out a timeline for a narrative paragraph and in Book 3, they complete a Venn diagram for a compare-contrast essay. In the final unit of Books 4 and 5, they use multiple organizers.

- *Sample paragraphs and essays* throughout the units, tied to the unit theme and writing assignments, provide clear models for students as they learn how to compose a topic sentence, thesis statement, introduction, body, and conclusion.

Carefully Targeted Grammar Instruction

Each unit in *Focus on Writing* helps students make the essential link between grammar and writing. The grammar topics for each unit are carefully chosen and correlated to *Focus on Grammar* to help students fulfill the writing goals of the unit.

Online Teacher's Manuals

The online Teacher's Manuals include model lesson plans, specific unit overviews, timed writing assignments, authentic student models for each assignment, rubrics targeted specifically for the writing assignment, and answer keys.

To the Student

Welcome to *Focus on Writing*! This book will help you develop your writing skills. You will learn about and practice the steps in the writing process.

All of the units are easy to follow. They include many examples, models, and of course, lots of writing activities.

Read the explanations on the next few pages before you begin Unit 1.

> Before you begin to write, you need to know what you will write about. To help you, you will see the **writing focus** under the title of the unit. A picture, a short reading and a **brainstorming** activity will help you get ideas about a topic. Putting your ideas into a **graphic organizer** will help you structure your ideas.

UNIT 2 Growing Up Too Fast?

IN THIS UNIT You will be writing a persuasive essay about whether or not it is a good idea for young children or teens to enter the professional world.

On May 22, 2010, at the age of 13, Jordan Romero became the youngest person ever to climb Mount Everest, the highest mountain peak in the world. He did not face this challenge alone. With him were a team of climbers, including his father and his stepmother. There were also three Sherpas, people in Nepal and Tibet who are famous for their mountaineering skills. Before and after this event, people around the world debated whether it was a good idea to let a young teenager attempt such a dangerous climb. What do you think?

Planning for Writing

■ BRAINSTORM

A. Look at this list of activities. Beside each activity, write the age at which you think it is OK for someone to do the activity for the first time. Put an X if you think the activity is not appropriate at any age. Then work with a partner. Discuss the reasons for your answers.

_____ 1. take public transportation alone

_____ 2. watch a violent movie

_____ 3. stay out with friends until midnight

_____ 4. get a part-time job

_____ 5. live away from the family

_____ 6. drink alcohol

_____ 7. babysit a younger sibling or neighbor

_____ 8. have a credit card

_____ 9. go out on a date

_____ 10. go to a dance club

_____ 11. join the military

_____ 12. take a vacation with friends

_____ 13. drop out of school

_____ 14. go hunting

_____ 15. get a pilot's license

_____ 16. go skydiving

B. Using a T-chart. As you learned in Unit 1, you can use a T-chart to list your thoughts about two sides of an issue.

Imagine that you are the parent of a 13-year-old who wants to climb Mount Everest, the world's highest mountain, with a team of experienced climbers. Before you decide if you should let your child go, consider the potential benefits and drawbacks. Share with a partner or work with a group.

Benefits (advantages)	Drawbacks (disadvantages)
He could become famous.	*He might have to face dangerous situations.*

27

A **reading** about the topic will help you develop more ideas. The reading can be a newspaper or magazine article, a webpage, or a blog.

Building Word Knowledge activities introduce a vocabulary or dictionary skill that you will be able to use when you write your assignment. For example, you will practice using different word forms and collocations.

A useful **Tip for Writers** gives you specific writing tools, for example, how to use descriptive details and when to use conjunctions to connect ideas.

■ READ

Read the online news article about Jordan Romero.

The Globe and Mail   April 29, 2010   By Hayley Mick

At 13, is Jordan Romero too young to climb Mount Everest?

1 *He's en route to potentially becoming the youngest to summit at Mount Everest, but some experts say the risks outweigh the reward.*

2 Jordan Romero recently finished his algebra homework in a tent located 6,500 metres above sea level.

3 The 13-year-old's social studies lessons on Mount Everest have been even more unorthodox[1] —ranging from meeting Nepalese girls to real-world applications of communications technology. "Hi Mom," he said, during a recent CNN interview broadcast from his tent.

4 In a month or so, the floppy-haired California teen plans to be the youngest person to climb the world's highest peak. His father, Paul Romero, and stepmother, Karen Lundgren, will guide him up another 2,300 metres from his current location at advanced base camp. "I think it's pretty responsible parenting," Mr. Romero said recently. "I'm taking my son around the world, trying to give him the best education, the best life experiences."

5 But what Jordan calls a dream come true is raising serious concerns within the climbing community. His case has already sparked[2] debate in mountaineering blogs and publications about how young is too young to climb. Some worry whether a 13-year-old can fully comprehend the risks he faces on a peak that has already claimed about 200 lives.

6 "He's got his whole life to climb Everest," said Todd Burleson, leader of eight expeditions and founder of a Seattle-based guide company and mountaineering school, Alpine Ascents International. "Being the youngest boy to climb is a fashionable, celebrity-oriented sort of thing. But it's not about [loving] the mountains. It's like trying to get your PhD at 10."

7 Jordan's father, a flight paramedic, and stepmother, a personal trainer, have no previous experience on Everest. Both are adventure racers, however. The trio has climbed several major peaks, including Kilimanjaro when Jordan was 9. The highest was Aconcagua in Argentina, which stands at about 7,000 metres.

8 For Everest, they have trained with hypoxic altitude tents[3] and hired Sherpas to accompany them to the 8,848-metre high peak on the border of China and Nepal. Mr. Romero has said he's confident in his decision to avoid the $65,000 (U.S.) fee for a professional guide. "We know when to step back, we know when to turn around," he told CNN.

9 But Mr. Burleson warns that Everest is unpredictable. Extreme heights and quickly changing weather can leave climbers vulnerable to frostbite, altitude sickness and death. "Let me tell you: The Himalayas are a whole other world," he said.

---

[1] **unorthodox:** unusual, not typical or traditional
[2] **sparked:** started, as with a first
[3] **hypoxic altitude tent:** a special tent used to train people to tolerate low oxygen levels at high altitudes

28   UNIT 2

---

7 The physical health effects of childhood obesity can be just as serious as the psychological ones. Common physical problems include cardiovascular diseases, such as heart failure[1] or stroke.[2] Childhood obesity can also increase someone's chances of getting Type 2 diabetes,[3] high blood pressure, and high cholesterol. It may also lead to sleep disorders, such as sleep apnea,[4] and eating disorders, such as anorexia nervosa. An obese child may also suffer from lack of stamina[5] and bone and joint problems.

8 If ignored, childhood obesity can develop into a life-threatening condition. Therefore, remember the saying "An ounce of prevention is worth a pound of cure." Steps need to be taken to ensure a healthy future for our children, including a healthy diet and proper exercise. Adults have the responsibility to guide and educate younger generations to make healthy choices. If you are not sure what is best for your child, get advice from a certified nutritionist or from your family doctor, but do not delay.

[1] **heart failure:** the inability of the heart to keep working effectively, which can cause death
[2] **stroke:** a sudden illness in which an artery (tube carrying blood) in the brain bursts or becomes blocked
[3] **Type 2 diabetes:** a lifelong disease caused by high levels of sugar (glucose) in the blood
[4] **sleep apnea:** pauses in breathing that interrupt sleep
[5] **stamina:** the ability to continue doing something without losing energy or interest

Building Word Knowledge

Using Word Forms. When you write, be sure to use the correct form of each word. Many English words have a variety of forms, including verb (v.), noun (n.), and adjective (adj.) forms. As you can see, sometimes the spelling changes and sometimes it does not.

Verb	Noun	Adjective
exercise	exercise	
	health	health healthy
	nutrient nutrition nutritionist	nutritional nutritious
	obesity	obese
overeat	overeater overeating	

Find forms of these words in the reading on page 4. Notice how they are used.

Focused Practice

A. *Read the Tip for Writers. Then identify the writer's main purpose for writing "An Ounce of Prevention." Circle the number of the statement that tells you.*

1. to persuade readers to support a ban on junk food in elementary and secondary school cafeterias

2. to persuade readers to teach children about the importance of exercise and eating healthful foods

(continued)

> **Tip for Writers**
>
> Good writers **determine their purpose for writing before they begin.** Their purpose, or reason, affects how and what they write. Three basic purposes for writing are to inform, to persuade, or to entertain.

Making Healthy Choices   **5**

■ STEP 1: PREWRITING

This section helps you further develop your ideas. It gives you a short explanation of the writing assignment. A small outline gives you a "picture" of the parts of the writing process.

The **Your Own Writing** section gives you a choice of two writing assignments. After you choose one of the assignments, you can begin to think about what you will write and share your ideas with a partner (**Checking in**). Finally, you will complete a **graphic organizer** with ideas for your own writing assignment.

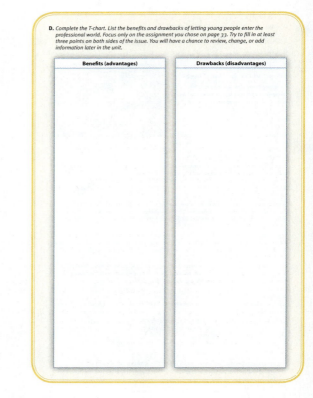

Step 1   Prewriting

For a persuasive essay, the first step is to select a topic that people have different opinions about. The prewriting step also includes considering various opinions and arguments about the topic before deciding on your opinion. As you decide on your own view or belief, be sure to consider the opposite points of view as well. It is important to think about why people might disagree with your argument.

Your Own Writing

Choosing Your Assignment

A. *Choose Assignment 1 or Assignment 2.*

1. Many teenagers play competitive sports from the time they are young children. Some start as young as five years old. Some even leave their homes and schools to join professional teams. Should exceptionally talented young athletes be allowed to play professional sports when they are still in their early teens even if it means they will have to move away from home and leave school? Write a persuasive essay that develops and supports your opinion on this issue.

2. Many people dream of becoming famous television or movie actors, and sometimes such fame begins at an early age. Child stars often get their education through private tutoring and have only limited opportunities for social interaction with other children outside of the acting profession. Should parents encourage their young children to become famous movie or television stars? Write a persuasive essay that develops and supports your opinion on this issue.

B. *Freewrite for ten minutes on your assignment. Here are some questions to get you started:*

• Why did you choose this assignment?

• What kind of life do you think a young person would have in an adult professional world? What would be some of the benefits? What would be some of the drawbacks?

• Have you ever known or heard about someone who had to make a similar choice?

• Why might someone disagree with your point of view?

• What more do you want to find out?

C. Checking in. *Work with a partner who chose the same assignment. Discuss the ideas and details you wrote in Exercise B. Ask your partner some questions about his or her topic. Did your partner . . .*

• express an opinion about what life would be like for a young person in a professional world?

• talk about benefits and drawbacks?

• consider other people's points of view?

Share your point of view about your partner's topic. Based on your discussion, make changes and additions to your writing.

Growing Up Too Fast? **33**

D. *Complete the T-chart. List the benefits and drawbacks of letting young people enter the professional world. Focus only on the assignment you chose on page 33. Try to fill in at least three points on both sides of the issue. You will have a chance to review, change, or add information later in the unit.*

Benefits (advantages)	Drawbacks (disadvantages)

34 UNIT 2

STEP 2: WRITING THE FIRST DRAFT

This section guides you through each part of your writing assignment. For a paragraph assignment, you will learn how to write a topic sentence, body sentences, and concluding sentence(s). For an essay assignment, you will learn how to write a thesis statement, introductory paragraph, body paragraph, and conclusion. At the end of Step 2, you will be able to write a complete first draft.

Focused Practice activities will give you lots of writing practice *before* you draft your writing assignment. Make sure to look at all of the examples and models before you complete the exercises. The outline of the parts of the writing assignment helps you to keep track of where you are in the process.

Step 2   Writing the First Draft

THE INTRODUCTION

The *introductory paragraph* of an academic essay contains two parts:

The Persuasive Essay

▼ Introduction
- Background Information
- Thesis Statement
  - Argument or Reasoning
  - Persuasive Language
▶ Body
▶ Conclusion

1. *Background information* about the topic of the essay helps your reader understand and become interested in the topic. Before you begin writing, ask yourself: *What important background information does my reader need to know?* or *What's the situation that I am writing about?* Do not give too many details—provide only what the reader needs.

2. The *thesis statement* presents the controlling idea of the essay. It may be one or two sentences. In a persuasive essay, your thesis statement will include your opinion or point of view on the issue. The thesis statement is typically the last sentence of the introductory paragraph.

In a persuasive essay, the background often includes opposing views people have about the issue. Then the thesis statement presents the writer's opinion or point of view. The thesis statement in a persuasive essay is similar to the topic sentence in a persuasive paragraph because you want to convince your reader to share your point of view. Therefore, your thesis statement should also have *persuasive language*—words and phrases that suggest that you are giving an opinion. You learned about some of these words and phrases in Unit 1. Other examples of persuasive language include:

I strongly believe that . . .	*It is a mistake to . . .*
It is irresponsible to . . .	*It is definitely the right decision to . . .*
It is a good idea to . . .	

Example:

background
↓

[Children are full of energy and ideas; however, their ideas don't always make sense. Sometimes their ideas might even be dangerous. The role of parents is to guide their children and, when necessary, to make proper decisions for their protection. This can be tricky. On the one hand, parents don't want to put their child in harm's way, but on the other hand, they don't want to step on their child's dreams either. Paul Romero faced such a challenge when his nine-year-old son, Jordan, expressed a desire to climb the Seven Summits, the highest peaks on each of the seven continents. I can appreciate his desire to educate his son and

thesis statement

help Jordan pursue his dreams.] [However, I strongly believe that Paul Romero's decision to allow Jordan to climb these mountains was foolish and irresponsible.]

▢ persuasive language	▢ issue	▢ opinion

Growing Up Too Fast?   35

Focused Practice

A. *Read the following essay assignment. Then combine each set of sentences below into two different topic sentences for a body paragraph, using the transition words. The first one is done for you.*

Do you agree or disagree with the decision to let Jordan Romero climb the Seven Summits?

1. Jordan should be encouraged to take these risks.
   He could make a lot of money for himself and his family.

   First, _Jordan Romero should be encouraged to take these risks because he could make a lot of money for himself and his family._

   The first reason _that Jordan should be encouraged to take these risks is that he could make a lot of money for himself and his family._

2. I think letting him climb Everest was a mistake.
   Mother Nature is too unpredictable.

   Another reason _____

   _____

   Additionally, _____

   _____

3. I think his father made the right decision.
   This is because it is a unique opportunity for Jordan to see the world.

   Most important, _____

   _____

   The most important reason _____

   _____

4. I disagree with the decision to let Jordan climb.
   He is not mature enough to make important decisions.

   Finally, _____

   _____

   The final reason _____

   _____

40   UNIT 2

STEP 3: REVISING

After you write your first draft, you aren't finished yet! Step 3 shows you how important it is to look again at your writing.

> Review and analyze the **model** paragraphs or essays to get an idea of what a well-written paragraph or essay looks like. You will see how the parts of your own writing should fit together.
>
> Completing the **Revision Checklists** for each writing assignment will help you identify parts of your draft that need improvement.

Step 3   Revising

Revising your work is an essential part of the writing process. This is your opportunity to be sure that your essay has all the important pieces and that it is clear.

Focused Practice

A. *You have read parts of this persuasive essay already. Now read the entire essay to see how the parts fit together.*

A Parent's Job Is to Protect

Children are full of energy and ideas; however, their ideas don't always make sense. Sometimes their ideas might even be dangerous. The role of parents is to guide their children and, when necessary, to make proper decisions for their protection. This can be tricky. On the one hand, parents don't want to put their child in harm's way, but on the other hand, they don't want to step on their child's dreams either. Paul Romero faced such a challenge when his nine-year-old son, Jordan, expressed a desire to climb the Seven Summits, the highest peaks on each of the seven continents. I can appreciate his desire to educate his son and help Jordan pursue his dreams. However, I strongly believe that Paul Romero's decision to allow Jordan to climb these mountains, and especially Mt. Everest, was foolish and irresponsible.

First of all, his family should not have let him climb because he is physically too young to do it. Even though at 5'8" and 140 pounds, he is above average for a 13-year-old boy, his body is still growing. His bones and muscles are still growing and his brain is still developing. Researchers are not sure about the effect of high altitudes on teenagers because they have not studied teens specifically. Some say it can cause long-term brain damage. The article, "At 13, is Jordan Romero too young to climb Mount Everest?" quotes a leading authority on altitude sickness, Peter Hackett. He said that some researchers believe that a young brain is more resilient than an adult brain, but others argue that the brains of the young are more vulnerable. Clearly the research is not conclusive. However, I don't understand why a parent would put a growing child at risk in this way.

Another reason why I think the decision was wrong is that Mother Nature is too unpredictable. We have seen the destructive potential of storms such as Hurricane Katrina in New Orleans, Louisiana. Even specialists could not handle or control the effects of that storm. How will a 13-year-old make the tough decisions

(continued)

---

6. Eventually I want to run my own business, but for now my _____ is to get work experience and save some money.

7. If you buy a jacket and then decide that you don't like it, you can return it the next day for a _____ or a store credit.

8. It's very difficult for families to save enough money to pay their children's _____. Scholarships and student loans may help.

9. My _____ is going really well. I have three interviews next week.

Your Own Writing

Revising Your Draft

A. *Reread the first draft of your essay. Use the Revision Checklist to identify parts of your writing that might need improvement.*

B. *Review your plans and notes and your responses to the Revision Checklist. Then revise your first draft. Save your revised essay. You will look at it again in the next section.*

Revision Checklist

Did you . . .

- ☐ identify and explain the problem in the introduction?
- ☐ include a thesis statement that restates the problem and proposes a solution?
- ☐ clearly show why the problem is serious in the first body paragraph?
- ☐ propose and explain at least one solution?
- ☐ offer supporting examples, facts, or comments from experts?
- ☐ return to the main idea in your thesis statement to signal the end of your essay?
- ☐ use a concluding strategy to end your essay?
- ☐ use collocations correctly?
- ☐ give your essay an interesting title?

■ STEP 4: EDITING

In the final step, you review a grammar topic that will help you edit your revised draft. Then you use an Editing Checklist to correct your own paragraph or essay for any errors in grammar, punctuation, or spelling.

Grammar Presentation charts present notes and examples on specific grammar topics related to your writing assignment. Then you follow up with grammar practice.

Editing Checklists for each writing assignment help you correct and polish your final draft.

Step 4 Editing

■ GRAMMAR PRESENTATION

Before you hand in your revised essay, you must check it for any errors in grammar, punctuation, and spelling. In this section you will learn about the verbs *make, have, let, help,* and *get*. You will focus on this grammar when you edit and proofread your essay.

Make, Have, Let, Help, and Get

Grammar Notes	Examples
1. Use *make, have* and *get* to talk about things that one person causes another person to do. These verbs show how much choice the other person has about doing the action	
a. *make* + object + base form of the verb often means to force a person to do something. There is no choice.	*less choice* • His parents didn't **make** *him* **climb** Everest. He wanted to do it.
b. *have* + object + base form of the verb often means to cause a person to do a task. There is some choice.	• The climbers didn't carry their luggage and supplies. They **had** *the porters* **carry** them.
c. *get* + object + infinitive often means to persuade a person to do something by giving rewards or good reasons. There is a choice.	• Paul Romero **got** *his son* **to do** his algebra homework by threatening to cancel the climb up Everest. *more choice*
Be Careful! *Get* is always followed by **object + infinitive**, NOT the base form of the verb.	NOT: Team Romero got Sherpas ~~carry~~ their luggage and supplies.
Make can also mean to have an effect on something or someone.	• The high altitude **made** *the climbers* **feel** sick.
2. *Let* + object + base form of the verb means to allow a person to do something. Be Careful! *Allow* is followed by **object + infinitive**, NOT the base form of the verb.	• How can parents **let** *their child* **do** something so dangerous? • How can parents **allow** *their children* **to do** something so dangerous? NOT: How can parents allow their children ~~do~~ something so dangerous?
3. *Help* means to make something easier for a person. Help can be followed by: **object + base form of the verb** OR **object + infinitive** The meaning is the same.	• Paul Romero **is helping** *Jordan* **follow** his dreams. OR • Paul Romero **is helping** *Jordan* **to follow** his dreams.

Growing Up Too Fast? **53**

E. *Write five sentences related to the assignment you chose on page 99. Use adjective clauses. These may be sentences you already have in your essay.*

1. _____
   _____

2. _____
   _____

3. _____
   _____

4. _____
   _____

5. _____
   _____

Your Own Writing
Editing Your Draft

A. *Use the Editing Checklist to edit and proofread your essay.*

B. *Prepare a clean copy of the final draft of your essay and hand it in to your teacher.*

Editing Checklist
Did you . . . ☐ include adjective clauses and use them correctly? ☐ use correct verb forms, punctuation, and spelling? ☐ use "new words" and other words correctly?

Then and Now **121**

Now, you are ready to begin with Unit 1. Enjoy the writing process!

Scope and Sequence

UNIT	STEP 1 Planning and Prewriting	STEP 2 Writing the First Draft
1 Making Healthy Choices ***Writing Focus*** Writing a persuasive paragraph ***Reading*** *An Ounce of Prevention,* an article about preventing childhood obesity	Using a T-chart Identifying word forms Determining the purpose Choosing a writing assignment for a persuasive paragraph Freewriting about the topic Sharing points of view	Writing a topic sentence with a controlling idea and an opinion Using persuasive language Researching the topic and taking notes Giving reasons and examples Using facts and information from experts Using listing order transition words Restating the controlling idea and using concluding strategies
2 Growing Up Too Fast? ***Writing Focus*** Writing a persuasive essay ***Reading*** *At 13, is Jordan Romero too young to climb Mount Everest?,* an article about a teenage explorer	Using a T-chart Identifying word forms Identifying the audience Distinguishing between a paragraph and an essay Choosing a writing assignment for a persuasive essay Freewriting about the topic Sharing points of view	Providing background information for a persuasive essay Writing thesis statements that express an opinion Using persuasive language Researching the topic and taking notes Writing topic sentences Using transition words to give reasons Developing and supporting a point of view with facts, explanations, and anecdotes Restating the thesis and using concluding strategies
3 Being Part of the Solution ***Writing Focus*** Writing a problem-solution essay ***Reading*** *Is Cash the Answer?* an excerpt from a magazine article about paying kids to do well in school	Using a problem-solution chart Using collocations Being aware of opposing points of view Choosing a writing assignment for a problem-solution essay Freewriting about the topic Sharing opinions	Providing background information for a problem-solution essay Writing thesis statements that state problems and hint at or state solutions Researching the topic and taking notes Writing topic sentences Developing and supporting a proposed solution with facts or comments from experts Using transitions to connect paragraphs Restating the thesis and using a concluding strategy

STEP 3 Revising	STEP 4 Editing	Learning Outcome	*Focus on Grammar Level 4, Fourth Edition*
Analyzing a model paragraph Identifying word forms Applying the Revision Checklist and writing the second draft	Reviewing simple present, present perfect, and simple past Incorporating the grammar in sentences Editing a paragraph for grammatical correctness Applying the Editing Checklist and writing the final draft	Can develop clear paragraphs expanding and supporting the main points with relevant details and examples. Can explain the advantages and disadvantages of various options.	**Unit 1** Simple Present and Present Progressive **Unit 2** Simple Past and Past Progressive **Unit 3** Simple Past, Present Perfect, and Present Perfect Progressive
Analyzing a model persuasive essay Writing sentences with correct word forms Applying the Revision Checklist and writing a second draft	Reviewing *make, have, let, help,* and *get* Incorporating the grammar in sentences Editing a paragraph for grammatical correctness Applying the Editing Checklist and writing the final draft	Can write essays that develop an argument giving reasons in support of or against a particular point of view. Can write clear, detailed essays in an assured, personal, natural style targeted to a specific audience.	**Unit 10** *Make, Have, Let, Help,* and *Get*
Analyzing a model problem-solution essay Using collocations in sentences Applying the Revision Checklist and writing the second draft	Reviewing modals Incorporating the grammar in sentences Editing a paragraph for grammatical correctness Applying the Editing Checklist and writing the final draft	Can write essays that evaluate different ideas or solutions to a problem. Can check information and explain problems with reasonable precision.	**Unit 15** Modals and Similar Expressions

UNIT	STEP 1 Planning and Prewriting	STEP 2 Writing the First Draft
4 Then and Now ***Writing Focus*** Writing a compare-contrast essay ***Reading*** *Talk of The Times: The Good Old Days*, a blog about adapting to change	Using a compare-contrast chart Using new words Using various levels of formality in writing Choosing a writing assignment for a compare-contrast essay Freewriting about the topic Sharing ideas and details about two inventions or events	Providing background information for a compare-contrast essay Identifying points of comparison Writing thesis statements that give points of comparison Researching the topic and taking notes Writing topic sentences with transition words and phrases that show addition and contrast Using the block or point-by-point method Restating the thesis and using concluding strategies
5 Happiness ***Writing Focus*** Writing a cause-effect essay ***Reading*** *Happiness May Come with Age*, an article about research on happiness and aging	Using a cause-effect web Using reporting verbs Using reliable sources Choosing a writing assignment for a cause-effect essay Freewriting about the topic Sharing points of view	Providing background information for a cause-effect essay Writing thesis statements that focus on causes or effects Researching the topic and taking notes Writing topic sentences Paraphrasing others' ideas Crediting sources Using transitions to connect body paragraphs Restating the thesis and using concluding strategies
6 What to Do? ***Writing Focus*** Writing an essay with two or more structures ***Reading*** *Ethics 101*, a professor's lecture notes and assignment	Using a T-chart, problem-solution chart, or cause-effect web Using idioms Choosing an organizational structure to accomplish the purpose for writing Choosing a writing assignment for an essay with multiple structures Freewriting about the topic Sharing points of view on the topic	Using an opening strategy to stimulate interest Providing background information Writing thesis statements that express opinions Researching the topic and taking notes Using various organizational structures to support the thesis Using words and phrases to signal a particular rhetorical structure Restating the thesis and using concluding strategies

STEP 3 Revising	STEP 4 Editing	Learning Outcome	*Focus on Grammar Level 4, Fourth Edition*
Analyzing a model compare-contrast essay Writing definitions for new words Applying the Revision Checklist and writing the second draft	Reviewing adjective clauses Incorporating the grammar in sentences Editing a paragraph for grammatical correctness Applying the Editing Checklist and writing the final draft	Can write clear, well-structured essays on complex subjects. Can expand and support ideas at some length with additional points, reasons, and relevant examples.	**Unit 13** Adjective Clauses with Subject Relative Pronouns **Unit 14** Adjective Clauses with Object Relative Pronouns or *When* and *Where*
Analyzing a model cause-effect essay Using reporting verbs in sentences Applying the Revision Checklist and writing the second draft	Reviewing direct and indirect speech Incorporating the grammar in sentences Editing a report for grammatical correctness Applying the Editing Checklist and writing the final draft	Can write essays that convey information and ideas on abstract as well as concrete topics. Can summarize extracts from news items, interviews containing opinions, argument, and discussion. Can synthesize information and arguments from a number of sources.	**Unit 25** Direct and Indirect Speech
Analyzing a model essay with two or more structures Using idioms in conversational sentences Applying the Revision Checklist and writing the second draft	Reviewing real and unreal conditionals Incorporating the grammar in sentences Editing sentences for grammatical correctness Applying the Editing Checklist and writing the final draft	Can produce clear, smoothly flowing, complex essays that present a case. Can provide an appropriate and effective logical structure that helps the reader to find significant points.	**Unit 21** Present Real Conditionals **Unit 22** Future Real Conditionals **Unit 23** Present and Future Unreal Conditionals

Making Healthy Choices

UNIT 1

IN THIS UNIT   You will be writing a persuasive paragraph about childhood obesity.

People come in all different shapes and sizes. This diversity is something to celebrate. However, sometimes a person can become so overweight that it becomes a serious health problem. Being overweight is particularly dangerous for children. Today, in many parts of the world, childhood obesity—a condition in which a child's weight is far above the average range for his or her age, height, and gender—has become a public health crisis. To reverse the trend toward childhood obesity, there has been increasing research into its causes, effects, and prevention. What steps do you think can be taken to fight childhood obesity?

Planning for Writing

■ BRAINSTORM

A. *Work with a partner. What are some causes of childhood obesity? What are some problems a child might have as a result of being obese? List them. Then discuss your lists with another pair. Which do you think are the three most serious causes?*

Causes	Problems
overeating at meals	*high blood pressure*

B. *Junk food is usually tasty and inexpensive. However, it is low in nutritional value and contains a lot of sugar and/or fat. List some kinds of junk food that you know. Then check (✓) the items that are usually available to children in school cafeterias.*

	donuts		
✓	*French fries*		

C. **Using a T-Chart.** You can use a two-column graphic organizer, or T-chart, like the one below to look at two sides of an issue. You can list reasons that support the issue on one side of the chart and reasons that oppose the issue on the other side.

Your city has proposed banning junk food from all school cafeterias. Complete the T-chart. Add three reasons to each side of the chart. Then discuss your chart with a partner.

Issue: *Banning junk food from school cafeterias*	
Reasons for the Ban	**Reasons against the Ban**
• Schools should not support unhealthy eating habits.	• Students should be able to spend their money the way they want to.

AN OUNCE OF PREVENTION

By Richard Aquilina   Gohealthy.com

1   How often have you seen the picture of a baby and noticed how round or "pudgy" the baby is? Cute, right? Most of us start out life with a little baby fat, and that's OK. But what happens when this baby fat doesn't go away? What if, because of diet and lifestyle, children become overweight and stay that way?

2   Today, most people know that being overweight at a young age can lead to serious health problems. The simple fact is that overeating—eating more than the body needs—and lack of exercise can cause obesity in growing children. Still, the number of obese children is increasing at an alarming rate. Parents and teachers must learn how to prevent childhood obesity and the health problems associated with it.

3   One cause of excessive weight gain in children is the way people live these days. People in many modern cultures have very busy lifestyles. They rarely have or take the time to prepare healthy meals or do daily exercise. Research has shown that when people sit down at the table with family members for regular meals, they tend to be healthier. Despite this evidence, high-fat, high-calorie fast food and processed food often replace the home-cooked sit-down family meal. Children often prefer pizza and burgers to more nutritious choices. Junk foods, which contain a lot of fat and sugar but little nutritional value, can lead to excessive weight gain. Schools are not always helpful either. Cafeteria food in some schools is often no healthier than fast food. Furthermore, school and college vending machines that sell candy, potato chips, and sugary drinks also tempt young people looking for a quick fix for their hunger.

4   In addition, lack of sufficient physical activity adds to the problem. How ironic that in spite of our busy lives, we are less physically active than ever. With the popularity of computers, video games, and online communication children today are less likely to be outside playing and running around than they were in earlier generations. Schools have even cut down on physical education classes in order to give students more time in the classroom. This lack of physical activity is very harmful because it can lead to weight gain and obesity.

5   Lastly, family also plays a vital role in determining body type. Statistics show that there is an 80 percent chance of a child's becoming obese if both parents are obese and a 40 percent chance if one of the parents is obese. For this reason, the lessons about making healthy food choices need to start at home.

6   The effects of obesity in children can be divided into two categories: psychological and physical. The psychological effects can include poor self-esteem, depression, inability to form close relationships with family and friends, and fear of being laughed at or bullied. Obesity can cause a child to withdraw from healthy social activity. This isolation may, in turn, lead to other problems down the road, such as drug or alcohol abuse. These psychological effects, which show up at an early age, can have a serious impact well into adulthood.

7 The physical health effects of childhood obesity can be just as serious as the psychological ones. Common physical problems include cardiovascular diseases, such as heart failure[1] or stroke.[2] Childhood obesity can also increase someone's chances of getting Type 2 diabetes,[3] high blood pressure, and high cholesterol. It may also lead to sleep disorders, such as sleep apnea,[4] and eating disorders, such as anorexia nervosa. An obese child may also suffer from lack of stamina[5] and bone and joint problems.

8 If ignored, childhood obesity can develop into a life-threatening condition. Therefore, remember the saying "An ounce of prevention is worth a pound of cure." Steps need to be taken to ensure a healthy future for our children, including a healthy diet and proper exercise. Adults have the responsibility to guide and educate younger generations to make healthy choices. If you are not sure what is best for your child, get advice from a certified nutritionist or from your family doctor, but do not delay.

---

[1] **heart failure:** the inability of the heart to keep working effectively, which can cause death
[2] **stroke:** a sudden illness in which an artery (tube carrying blood) in the brain bursts or becomes blocked
[3] **Type 2 diabetes:** a lifelong disease caused by high levels of sugar (glucose) in the blood
[4] **sleep apnea:** pauses in breathing that interrupt sleep
[5] **stamina:** the ability to continue doing something without losing energy or interest

Building Word Knowledge

Using Word Forms. When you write, be sure to use the correct form of each word. Many English words have a variety of forms, including verb (v.), noun (n.), and adjective (adj.) forms. As you can see, sometimes the spelling changes and sometimes it does not.

Verb	Noun	Adjective
exercise	exercise	
	health	health healthy
	nutrient nutrition nutritionist	nutritional nutritious
	obesity	obese
overeat	overeater overeating	

Find forms of these words in the reading on page 4. Notice how they are used.

Focused Practice

A. *Read the* **Tip for Writers.** *Then identify the writer's main purpose for writing "An Ounce of Prevention." Circle the number of the statement that tells you.*

1. to persuade readers to support a ban on junk food in elementary and secondary school cafeterias

2. to persuade readers to teach children about the importance of exercise and eating healthful foods

(continued)

> ### Tip for Writers
>
> Good writers **determine their purpose for writing before they begin**. Their purpose, or reason, affects how and what they write. Three basic purposes for writing are to inform, to persuade, or to entertain.

3. to entertain people who enjoy reading about good food and cooking

4. to inform readers about the kinds of food they should be eating

5. to inform readers about common diseases that affect obese children

B. *"An Ounce of Prevention" discusses some of the causes and effects (results) of childhood obesity. Read each item in the chart. According to the article, is the item a cause or an effect? Put a check (✓) in the correct column.*

	Cause	Effect	Factors
1.			Avoiding social interaction
2.			Busy lifestyle
3.			Depression
4.			Sleep disorders
5.			Families not eating together
6.			Fast food or junk food
7.			Fear of being disliked or bullied by other kids
8.			High blood pressure or heart failure
9.			High-calorie foods
10.			High cholesterol
11.			Lack of physical activity
12.			Lack of stamina
13.			Poor food choices
14.			Possible drug or alcohol abuse
15.			Type 2 diabetes

C. *The title of the reading "An Ounce of Prevention" comes from the saying, "An ounce of prevention is worth a pound of cure." Work with a partner. Discuss the meaning of the saying. Why do you think the writer used it in the title and the reading? Then, on your own, write your ideas in three or four sentences.*

1 ounce (oz) = .03 kg
1 pound (lb) = .45 kg

_____

_____

_____

_____

_____

_____

_____

Writing a Persuasive Paragraph

In this unit, you are going to write a persuasive paragraph. When you write to persuade, you give one clear opinion about a debatable or controversial issue and try to convince the reader to share your point of view. Much academic writing—the writing you do in school—will be persuasive writing.

Like all academic paragraphs, a persuasive paragraph contains three parts.

> **The Persuasive Paragraph**
>
> ▶ Topic Sentence
> ▶ Body Sentences
> ▶ Concluding Sentence(s)

Step 1   Prewriting

For a persuasive paragraph, the prewriting step includes brainstorming various opinions and arguments about an issue. It also involves looking carefully at both sides of the issue before taking a position for or against it.

Your Own Writing

Choosing Your Assignment

A. *Choose Assignment 1 or Assignment 2.*

  1. Because of the alarming rate of childhood obesity and the power of advertising to attract children, a growing number of people think that junk food advertising should be banned or limited in some way. Would you be for or against such a ban? Write a persuasive paragraph in which you develop and support your position on this issue.

  2. Because of the high cost of health care and the number of medical problems related to childhood obesity, some people think that the government should impose a "junk food tax" on unhealthy or nonnutritious foods, such as sugary drinks and junk fast food. Would you be for or against such a tax? Write a persuasive paragraph in which you develop and support your position on this issue.

B. *Freewrite for ten minutes on your assignment. Here are some questions to get you started:*

  • What do you know or believe about junk food? Do you ever eat it? What kind(s) do you eat?

  • What are your initial opinions about the issue? Why do you feel this way? Who might disagree with you? Why?

  • What more might you need to find out in order to write a persuasive paragraph about the topic?

➡

C. Checking in. *Work with a partner who chose the same assignment. Discuss the topic and details you wrote in Exercise B. Ask your partner some questions about his or her topic. Did your partner . . .*

- express his or her knowledge and beliefs about junk food?

- explain reasons to be for or against it?

- explain who might disagree and why?

Share your own opinion about the topic. Based on your discussion, make changes and additions to your writing.

D. *Complete the T-chart. List the reasons for and against a ban on ads or a tax on junk food. Be sure to complete both sides of the chart. Fill in as much information as you can. You will have a chance to review, change, or add information later in the unit.*

Issue: _____	
Reasons for	**Reasons against**

■ THE TOPIC SENTENCE

The topic sentence of a paragraph presents the topic—who or what the paragraph is about—and the controlling idea about it. The controlling idea is the single point the writer is making about the topic. The topic sentence often comes at the beginning of an academic paragraph.

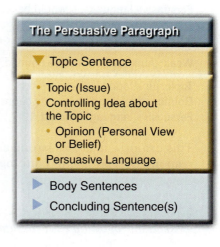

In a persuasive paragraph, the topic is usually an *issue* about which people have different opinions or points of view. The controlling idea is a specific *opinion* on that topic, or issue. In a persuasive paragraph, your topic sentence will state the personal belief or idea you have about an issue.

Remember that an *opinion* is different from a *fact*. A fact gives information that can be proven and measured. Most people agree that a fact is true. An opinion is a personal belief or point of view. Notice the difference between fact and opinion in the example below.

Example:

Fact: There is often a lot of junk food in school cafeterias and vending machines.
Opinion: Junk food should be banned from school cafeterias.

A topic sentence in a persuasive paragraph also includes *persuasive language*. Persuasive language consists of words and phrases that suggest the writer is giving an opinion. Some writers use expressions such as *In my opinion . . .* , *I believe . . .* or *I think . . .*

Here are some other examples of persuasive language.

Persuasive Language	
Modal Verbs	**Expressions**
should have to need to must	Without a doubt . . . It would be a mistake (not) to . . . There can be no denying (the fact) that . . .

When you read the following assignment for a persuasive paragraph and the topic sentences, you can see the differences between the two strong topic sentences and the weak one.

> *Considering the many problems that result from childhood obesity, should junk food be banned from schools?*

Examples:

Strong: I believe junk food should be banned from schools in order to protect children's health.

Topic: Junk food in schools
Opinion: It should be banned to protect children's health.
Persuasive Language: I believe, should

This is a strong topic sentence because it states the topic and uses persuasive language to express an opinion about it.

Strong: It would be a serious mistake to allow schools to continue serving unhealthy food to young children.

Topic: unhealthy food in schools
Opinion: Schools shouldn't be allowed to serve unhealthy food.
Persuasive language: It would be a serious mistake . . .

This is also a strong topic sentence. It has all of the essential parts.

Weak: Junk food should be banned.

Topic: junk food
Opinion: Junk food should be banned.
Persuasive language: should

This example is not as strong as the first two examples because it doesn't completely respond to the topic of banning junk food *in schools*.

Focused Practice

A. *Read the following essay assignment. Then choose the topic sentence that best completes the paragraph. Write the topic sentence on the lines. Discuss your answer with a partner. Give reasons for your choice if you and your partner have different opinions.*

Considering the many problems that result from childhood obesity, should junk food be banned from schools?

Ban It Now!

_____

_____ Sugar makes children very active, even hyperactive, because their blood sugar levels increase rapidly. However, when the sugar runs out, they eventually "crash." That is, they lose all of their energy— and more. As a result of feeling so tired, they may then feel the need for more sugary food to get their energy back up. This becomes an unhealthy cycle. Under these circumstances, students have a hard time focusing on their schoolwork, their homework, and exams. Why would we want to encourage something that is standing in the way of students doing well in school? We need to stop this cycle early on so that it doesn't continue.

---

1. Companies that make or sell junk food to our children are making a lot of money, and they should be stopped.

2. I strongly believe that junk food, especially sugary snacks and drinks, should be taken out of schools immediately.

3. School cafeterias should no longer be allowed to sell unhealthy food to students.

4. There can be no denying the fact that sugar has little nutritional value.

B. *Write one topic sentence with the topic, opinion, and persuasive language in each set.*

Considering the many problems that result from childhood obesity, should junk food be banned from schools?

1. *I don't think junk food should be banned from schools.*

   Topic: Junk food
   Opinion: Don't ban it from schools.
   Persuasive Language: I don't think / should

2. _____

   Topic: Junk food
   Opinion: We should ban it from schools.
   Persuasive Language: I believe / definitely

3. _____

   Topic: Junk food
   Opinion: Ban it from schools because such foods can cause serious health problems.
   Persuasive Language: should

4. _____

   Topic: Junk food
   Opinion: Don't ban it from schools. Students are responsible enough to make their own choices.
   Persuasive Language: should

5. _____

   Topic: Banning junk food
   Opinion: The parents association at this school want a ban. They say it will prevent children from becoming overweight and from developing health problems in the future.
   Persuasive Language: believe

6. _____

   Topic: Banning junk food from schools
   Opinion: It is another example of the government trying to take away individual freedom and, therefore, it is ridiculous.
   Persuasive Language: Without a doubt

7. _____

   Topic: Junk food in schools
   Opinion: It can be unhealthy for people if they eat too much. Therefore, ban it.
   Persuasive Language: I strongly believe / should

8. _____

   Topic: Junk food
   Opinion: Ban it in elementary and high schools, not in colleges.
   Persuasive Language: While I agree . . . / should / don't need to

Your Own Writing

Finding Out More

A. *You may want to learn more about the topic you chose on page 7. Review the guidelines for researching a topic in the Appendix on pages 188–189.*

- If you chose Assignment 1, go online or to the library to research the topic of banning junk food advertising. Look for reasons and examples of why banning junk food ads is good or bad. You may want to use the following keywords when you search for information online: *junk food, advertising, children,* and *ban.*

- If you chose Assignment 2, go online or to the library to research imposing taxes on unhealthy foods such as fried foods, sugary sodas, and juices. Find reasons and examples of why such a tax would be good or bad. You may want to use the following keywords when you search for information online: *junk food, soda, sugar,* and *tax.*

B. *Take notes about what you found out. Write down key information or quotations from experts on the topic. List reasons why people are in favor of or against a ban on advertising or tax on junk food. Note the sources for your information.*

C. Checking in. *Share your information with a partner. Did your partner . . .*

- gather enough information that is directly related, or relevant, to the issue? How do you know?

- use at least three reliable sources? Why or why not?

- find interesting reasons and examples to support his or her opinion? What are they?

Use this information when you write your essay.

Planning Your Topic Sentence

A. *Write a draft of your topic sentence. First, list the topic (issue), controlling idea (opinion), and persuasive language that you can use. Look back at your freewriting and T-chart to help you.*

Topic: _____

Controlling Idea about the Topic: _____

Persuasive Language: _____

Topic Sentence: _____

_____

B. Checking in. *Share your topic sentence with a partner. Did your partner . . .*

- clearly state the topic? If so, what is the topic?

- clearly express his or her opinion about the topic?

- use persuasive language?

C. *Tell your partner what you like about his or her topic sentence. If you have any suggestions for improving it, share them.*

D. *Based on your partner's feedback, you may want to rewrite your topic sentence.*

■ THE BODY SENTENCES

In the body sentences of a persuasive paragraph, you develop and support your controlling idea, or point of view, by giving and explaining the reasons for your opinion. For each reason, you should provide examples or other supporting details to show your readers why you think the way you do and to persuade them to accept your view. Use transition words to help readers understand the connection between your reasons and supporting details.

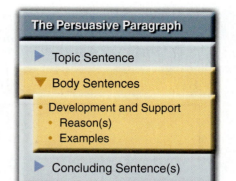

Giving Reasons and Examples

In a persuasive paragraph, it is important to give reasons to explain your point of view. For example, if you are writing about why serving junk food to children is harmful, you might give two reasons: (1) it makes them sluggish or tired and (2) it promotes unhealthy eating habits for the future. When you write your persuasive paragraph, you might introduce each reason with a listing-order transition word: *first*, *second*, *furthermore*, or *finally*. It may take you two or more sentences to clearly and completely explain each reason.

After giving a reason, support it with examples and other supporting details, such as with facts and information from experts on the topic or with an anecdote—a brief story from your personal experience. Strong examples and supporting details help readers to better understand your point of view and make it more convincing. For example, if you want to support the first reason above, that junk food makes students sluggish, give facts or other information from researchers who have studied this phenomenon. You could also write about your own or someone else's experience of feeling sluggish after eating junk food.

When you read the following essay assignment and the persuasive paragraph, you will see how the writer develops and supports a clear point of view.

> *Considering the many problems that result from childhood obesity, should junk food be banned from schools?*

Example:

Topic Sentence: There can be no doubt that a ban on junk food in school cafeterias should be imposed as soon as possible.

Reason 1: First, if schools continue to serve students processed food or snacks high in sugar, students will not be in top condition to perform well in the classroom.
Example (information from experts): Phyllis Kramer, a nutritionist and author of the book *Nutrition for Life*, points out that children who do not get proper nutrition do poorly on activities that require concentration. Compared with their peers who eat healthier meals, these students have shorter attention spans, score lower on exams, and are late or absent more often.

Reason 2: Furthermore, giving this food to kids is reinforcing a behavior that will have long-term consequences. The eating habits we develop as children stay with us into adulthood.
Example (facts): According the National Heart Association, 40 percent of obese children and 70 percent of obese teens will become obese adults. This is dangerous because our chances of developing serious diseases, such as Type 2 diabetes and hypertension, increase if we eat a lot of junk food. These health problems may not appear when a person is young, but they may later on, and by then it may be too late.

Focused Practice

A. *Read the following essay assignment and the persuasive paragraphs. Then answer the questions.*

Considering the many problems that result from childhood obesity, should junk food be banned from schools?

1.

Healthy Habits

I think it is very important to ban junk food from elementary schools. First, it is critical that young children get into the habit of healthy eating as soon as possible. Of course, small kids love sugary drinks and candy, French fries, and soda. However, these foods and drinks are unhealthy and have none of the nutrition that children need for their growing bodies and brains. As nutrition specialists tell us, kids need a balance of fruits and vegetables, whole grains, dairy products such as yogurt, and lean meat and fish. These are the foods we need to serve in our schools. Furthermore, if elementary schools don't ban junk food from cafeterias and vending machines, students may become obese or develop health problems in the future. As adults, they will have a higher risk of heart attacks or high blood pressure. The National Heart Association reports that 40 percent of obese children and 70 percent of obese teens become obese adults and are at risk for high blood pressure and Type 2 diabetes. To prevent these problems, schools have to teach young children how to make healthy choices. We must stop tempting them with unhealthy choices in school cafeterias and vending machines. Unhealthy foods have no place in schools.

2.

A Ban for a Healthier Tomorrow

Junk food should be banned from elementary and secondary schools to promote better health for young people today and for their future. Adult behavior is often a direct reflection of what we were taught as children. We need to teach kids about proper nutrition before they develop unhealthy eating habits. For instance, my mother told me that she was an overweight child. Her parents thought that "plump" children looked healthier than skinny ones so they encouraged her to eat whatever she wanted and in generous portions. Needless to say, she quickly went from being plump to being obese. Today she still struggles with her weight, and she has high blood pressure. However, she knows that she has to take care of herself and set a good example for my sister and me. These days our family eats healthier food like lean meat and fish, vegetables, and whole-grain bread. She doesn't blame her parents for her current health because today we have much more information about nutrition. Young children should be eating whole grains, fiber, and low fat foods to have a healthy body and mind. If they do this, they will be able to study hard and become healthy eaters in the future. Therefore, we need to teach them early because bad habits are hard to break.

---

1. Underline the topic sentence in each paragraph. How does the writer feel about banning junk food in each one? _____

_____

2. How many reasons does the writer give in each paragraph?

Paragraph 1: _____

Paragraph 2: _____

3. What transition word(s), if any, does the writer use in each paragraph to introduce the reason(s)? Circle them.

4. What kinds of examples does the writer use in each paragraph to explain the reason(s)?

Paragraph 1: _____

Paragraph 2: _____

B. *Read the following essay assignment and the persuasive paragraph. Complete it by adding a second reason and supporting details. Then discuss your completed paragraph with a partner.*

Considering the many problems that result from childhood obesity, should junk food be banned from schools?

College Students Know Better

While banning junk food in elementary and secondary schools might make sense, I do not see any reason to do so in colleges. First, college students know what is healthy for them and what is not. By this time, they have probably taken nutrition classes that have taught them about the nutritious foods they need to be healthy and give them enough energy for the day. Physical education classes and school sports have also taught them the value of exercising and staying fit. Furthermore, their parents have told them about healthy eating habits. If they are lucky, they may also have seen advertising campaigns that promote healthy eating. Clearly college-aged students know how to make healthy choices. Second,

_____

_____

_____

_____

_____

_____ Frankly, it won't matter if they choose taste over nutrition once in a while. At some point we have to let them make their own choices. Part of growing up is making decisions. Therefore, a ban like this would be a mistake.

Your Own Writing

Planning Your Body Sentences

A. *Before you begin writing the body sentences for your paragraph, complete the outline. Copy your topic sentence from page 12.*

- List at least two main reasons for your opinion.

- Brainstorm specific examples or other supporting details to help illustrate each of your reasons.

Persuasive Paragraph

Topic Sentence: _____

_____

Reason: _____

Examples: _____

_____

_____

Reason: _____

Examples: _____

_____

_____

Reason: _____

Examples: _____

_____

_____

B. Checking in. *Share your outline with a partner. Did your partner . . .*

- provide reasons that clearly support the opinion?

- use convincing examples and supporting details?

- provide interesting supporting details?

C. *Based on your partner's feedback, you may want to rewrite parts of your outline.*

■ THE CONCLUDING SENTENCE(S)

The concluding sentences of a paragraph wrap up, or close, the discussion of your point of view. In this part of a paragraph, restate the controlling idea in the thesis statement. You can also use a concluding strategy to complete the paragraph.

Here are two strategies you might use to end your persuasive paragraph about childhood obesity.

1. Express a final thought or recommendation and what might happen if people follow (or do not follow) it.

2. Summarize the reasons you used to support your opinion.

Writers sometimes use transition words, such as *in conclusion, in summary, therefore,* or *finally* to signal to the reader that the paragraph is ending.

> **The Persuasive Paragraph**
>
> ▶ Topic Sentence
> ▶ Body Sentences
> ▼ Concluding Sentence(s)
> - Restatement of the Controlling Idea
> - Transition Words
> - Concluding Strategy

Focused Practice

Read the essay assignment and the persuasive paragraph. Choose the concluding sentences that best complete the paragraph. Write the sentences on the lines. Then answer the questions.

Considering the many problems that result from childhood obesity, should junk food be banned from colleges?

Making Choices

Junk food shouldn't be banned from college campuses because college students are more mature and they know how to make proper choices about what is good for them or not. Almost all college students know that a bowl of ice cream is full of calories, but has little nutrition. The information is right on the label. They are also aware of how nutritious salads can be. In addition, because they are more mature than younger students, college students may eat junk food but then balance it out with something healthier, like fruit. They might also find a way to burn the extra calories through exercise. _____

_____

_____

---

a. Therefore, junk food does not have to be banned from college cafeterias and vending machines. Banning junk food will only create more problems for students.

b. Lastly, college students very often balance what they eat. If they have a healthy breakfast, then it seems like having a less healthy lunch might not be such a serious problem.

c. Another reason colleges should not ban junk food is that college students do not have time to prepare healthy meals for themselves. They are too busy studying, going to class, and sometimes working to support themselves.

d. In conclusion, banning junk food from college campuses is not necessary. College students are old enough to know that they can balance their food choices and exercise in order to maintain good health.

1. Tell your partner why you chose your answer over the others.

2. Where does the writer return to the controlling idea in the topic sentence? Underline it.

3. Did the writer use a transition word or phrase in the concluding sentences? Circle it.

4. What concluding strategy did the writer use? _____

Your Own Writing

Planning Your Conclusion

A. *What transition word(s), if any, might you use to signal that your paragraph is ending? Check (✓) one.*

_____ In conclusion, . . .   _____ Therefore, . . .

_____ In summary, . . .   _____ Finally, . . .

B. *How will you rephrase your controlling idea in the conclusion? Write your idea here.*

_____

C. *What strategy from page 18 will you use to close the paragraph?*

_____

D. Checking in. *Share your ideas with a partner. Did your partner . . .*

• use a transition word to signal that the paragraph is ending?

• restate the controlling idea of the topic sentence in an interesting way?

• choose an effective concluding strategy?

Writing Your First Draft

Read the Tip for Writers. *Review your notes on pages 8, 12, and 17. Then write the first draft of your paragraph. When you are finished, give your paragraph a working title. Hand in your draft to your teacher.*

> **Tip for Writers**
>
> Remember that the **purpose** of every persuasive paragraph is to convince the reader to agree with your point of view.

Revising your work is an essential part of the writing process. This is your opportunity to be sure that your paragraph has all the important pieces and that it is clear.

Focused Practice

A. *Read the essay assignment and the persuasive paragraph.*

> *There is a proposal to allow Burger Queen, the fast food restaurant, to open a small takeout business in the student activities center at Clarke High School. Considering the many problems that result from childhood obesity, should Clarke High allow a fast food restaurant to open on campus?*

Give Us What We Want

Childhood obesity is certainly a problem that we need to address, but we do not need to ban Burger Queen from opening on campus. As a student, I see this issue differently from the nutritionists and parents who have voiced their opinions. First of all, you can't beat the cost of fast food. Most students in this school don't have a part-time job, and those who do have to watch what they spend. They can't afford special menu items. The salads and other nutritious items in the school cafeteria are typically one or two dollars more expensive. A meal at Burger Queen is simply more affordable. In addition to cost, we need to consider convenience. Students don't have a lot of time to eat. Usually at lunch or between classes there is just enough time for a quick bite of something. There is no time to stand in long cafeteria lines. They need to be able to buy something, sit down, and eat it before they have to run off to their next class. Burger Queen is designed to get customers in and out quickly. Finally, and perhaps most important, kids eat what they want to eat. They enjoy eating fast food even though it may not always be the healthiest choice. The fact is that fast food is more appealing to them. A warm hamburger is more satisfying than a cold salad. Fried chicken is tastier than baked chicken. French fries are more tempting than boiled vegetables. In conclusion, students need an opportunity to buy food that is economical, convenient, and enjoyable. Childhood obesity is a serious issue, but banning an on-campus Burger Queen is not the way to deal with it. Cost, time, and personal choice all need to be considered.

B. *Work with a partner. Answer the questions about the paragraph.*

1. What is the topic (issue) expressed in the topic sentence? Circle it.

2. What is the controlling idea (the opinion or point of view)? Underline it twice.

3. Did the writer use any persuasive language in the topic sentence to emphasize the opinion? Circle it.

4. What reasons did the paragraph include to explain the controlling idea? Underline the sentences that introduce the reasons.

5. What examples or supporting details does the writer use? Check the sentences that provide specific examples or supporting information.

6. What transition words does the writer use? Circle them.

7. Where does the writer restate the controlling idea? Underline it twice.

8. What concluding strategy did the writer use? Check (✓) one.

_____ Express a final thought or recommendation and what might happen if people follow (or do not follow) it.

_____ Summarize the reasons you used to support your opinion.

C. Checking in. *Discuss your marked-up paragraph with another pair of students. Then in your group, share one thing about the paragraph that you found the most interesting. Explain your answer.*

Building Word Knowledge

Using Word Forms. The writer of "Give Us What We Want" included different forms of certain words.

Read "Give Us What We Want" on page 4 again. Find the forms of the words afford, eat, health, nutrition, *and* obese.

- Write the forms of the words in the appropriate place on the chart based on how the writer used each one. The first one is done for you.

- Work with a partner and discuss your answers.

Verb	Noun	Adjective
afford		*affordable*

Your Own Writing

Revising Your Draft

A. *Reread the first draft of your paragraph. Use the Revision Checklist to identify parts of your writing that might need improvement.*

B. *Review your plans and notes and your responses to the Revision Checklist. Then revise your first draft. Save your revised paragraph. You will look at it again in the next section.*

Revision Checklist

Did you . . .

☐ present your topic and point of view in the topic sentence?

☐ use persuasive language in your topic sentence to emphasize your opinion?

☐ present two or three main reasons to support your opinion?

☐ provide specific examples or supporting details to illustrate each of your reasons?

☐ restate the controlling idea of your topic sentence in your conclusion?

☐ use transition words?

☐ use an effective concluding strategy?

☐ use various word forms correctly?

☐ have a clear purpose?

☐ give your paragraph an interesting title?

■ GRAMMAR PRESENTATION

Before you hand in your revised paragraph, you must check it for any errors in grammar, punctuation, and spelling. In this section, you will review some present and past verb forms. You will focus on this grammar when you edit and proofread your persuasive paragraph.

Review of the Simple Present, Present Perfect, and Simple Past

Grammar Notes	Examples
1. Use the **simple present** to describe what <u>generally happens</u> (but not necessarily right now).	• In school students **learn** about proper health and nutrition. • Lack of physical activity **adds** to the problem. • People **do not always have** time to prepare healthy meals.
2. Use the **present perfect** to describe actions that • started in the past but were <u>not completed</u>. • happened at some indefinite time in the past and <u>were completed</u>.	• Attitudes **have changed** because we understand the risks of being obese. • High calorie food **has replaced** a healthy diet. • I **haven't had** a hamburger in many years.
3. Use the **simple past** to describe an action that was <u>completed</u> at a specific time in the past. The simple past focuses on the <u>completion</u> of the past action. Regular verbs end in -ed. However, there are many common verbs that have irregular past forms. **NOTE:** The simple past focuses on the <u>completion</u> of the past action. We use the present perfect, (not the simple past), to show that the result of the action or state is <u>important in the present</u>. The present perfect always has some connection to the present.	REGULAR VERBS (-ed): • Last night I **asked** for a salad instead of French fries with my meal. • I **didn't ask** for a refill of my drink either. IRREGULAR VERBS: • When I **was** young, my family **ate** lots of vegetables and fish. • I **didn't eat** a lot of junk food when I was young. • Last night I **asked** for a salad instead of French fries with my meal. • I **have eaten** salads instead of French fries for several months.

Focused Practice

A. *Complete each sentence using the correct form of the verb in parentheses. The first one is done for you.*

1. As a child I ___*didn't mind*___ junk food advertising, but now as a parent, I
   (not mind)

   ___*think*___ it ___*is*___ a serious problem.
   (think)   **(be)**

2. These days, the average American _____ a gallon of soda a week,
   (drink)

   which _____ about 1,000 calories and no nutrition.
   (provide)

3. Since it _____ announced last week, the reaction against the
   (be)

   proposed soda tax _____ strong.
   (be)

4. When I _____ in elementary school, French fries _____
   (be)   **(be)**

   considered healthy because they _____ a kind of vegetable.
   (be)

5. By college, all students _____ about the value of a healthy diet.
   (hear)

   Therefore, I _____ that they _____ old enough to
   (think)   **(be)**

   decide for themselves.

6. Martin _____ with his weight for years. Last November, he
   (struggle)

   _____ one more fad diet that _____. Since then, he
   (try)   **(not work)**

   _____ five more pounds. He _____ really frustrated.
   (gain)   **(feel)**

B. *Read and edit the paragraph. There are seven errors in the use of the simple present, present perfect, or simple past. The first error has been corrected for you. Find and correct six more.*

A Ban Is Not the Answer

                    is

    Few people can deny that childhood obesity ~~has been~~ a serious problem

today, but banning nonnutritious food and sugary drinks from schools is not going

to solve the problem. Every time society had a problem, why do we have to pass

a law? It's crazy. This is just another example of how the government interferes

in our lives. The real problem is the everyday choices we made. We need to

teach children to make the right choices. A ban on junk food will take away their

freedom to choose. I have thought parents and teachers need to work together

to educate children about proper nutrition and then leave it up to individuals to

make the right decision for themselves. One hundred years ago, we haven't had

                                                      (continued)

---

the amount of legislation that we have today, but people still have happy lives back then. The government has to stop making so many laws. It needs to let people take responsibility for and accept the consequences of their choices. If parents and teachers do their jobs right, children will choose salad over French fries, grilled chicken over fried, and fresh fruit over candy bars. If kids didn't want it, then school cafeterias and fast food restaurants will stop trying to sell it to them.

C. *Write five sentences related to the assignment you chose on page 7. Use simple present, simple past, and present perfect. These may be sentences you already have in your paragraph.*

1. _____

_____

2. _____

_____

3. _____

_____

4. _____

_____

5. _____

_____

Your Own Writing

Editing Your Draft

A. *Use the Editing Checklist to edit and proofread your paragraph.*

B. *Prepare a clean copy of the final draft of your paragraph and hand it in to your teacher.*

Editing Checklist
Did you . . .
☐ use simple present, simple past, and present perfect verb forms correctly?
☐ use correct punctuation and spelling?
☐ use word forms correctly?

Growing Up Too Fast?

IN THIS UNIT You will be writing a persuasive essay about whether or not it is a good idea for young children or teens to enter the professional world.

On May 22, 2010, at the age of 13, Jordan Romero became the youngest person ever to climb Mount Everest, the highest mountain peak in the world. He did not face this challenge alone. With him were a team of climbers, including his father and his stepmother. There were also three Sherpas, people in Nepal and Tibet who are famous for their mountaineering skills. Before and after this event, people around the world debated whether it was a good idea to let a young teenager attempt such a dangerous climb. What do you think?

Planning for Writing

■ BRAINSTORM

A. Look at this list of activities. Beside each activity, write the age at which you think it is OK for someone to do the activity for the first time. Put an X if you think the activity is not appropriate at any age. Then work with a partner. Discuss the reasons for your answers.

_____ **1.** take public transportation alone

_____ **2.** watch a violent movie

_____ **3.** stay out with friends until midnight

_____ **4.** get a part-time job

_____ **5.** live away from the family

_____ **6.** drink alcohol

_____ **7.** babysit a younger sibling or neighbor

_____ **8.** have a credit card

_____ **9.** go out on a date

_____ **10.** go to a dance club

_____ **11.** join the military

_____ **12.** take a vacation with friends

_____ **13.** drop out of school

_____ **14.** go hunting

_____ **15.** get a pilot's license

_____ **16.** go skydiving

B. Using a T-chart. As you learned in Unit 1, you can use a T-chart to list your thoughts about two sides of an issue.

Imagine that you are the parent of a 13-year-old who wants to climb Mount Everest, the world's highest mountain, with a team of experienced climbers. Before you decide if you should let your child go, consider the potential benefits and drawbacks. Share with a partner or work with a group.

Benefits (advantages)	Drawbacks (disadvantages)
He could become famous.	He might have to face dangerous situations.

■ READ

Read the online news article about Jordan Romero.

The Globe and Mail   April 29, 2010   By Hayley Mick

At 13, is Jordan Romero too young to climb Mount Everest?

1   *He's en route to potentially becoming the youngest to summit at Mount Everest, but some experts say the risks outweigh the reward.*

2   Jordan Romero recently finished his algebra homework in a tent located 6,500 metres above sea level.

3   The 13-year-old's social studies lessons on Mount Everest have been even more unorthodox[1] —ranging from meeting Nepalese girls to real-world applications of communications technology. "Hi Mom," he said, during a recent CNN interview broadcast from his tent.

4   In a month or so, the floppy-haired California teen plans to be the youngest person to climb the world's highest peak. His father, Paul Romero, and stepmother, Karen Lundgren, will guide him up another 2,300 metres from his current location at advanced base camp. "I think it's pretty responsible parenting," Mr. Romero said recently. "I'm taking my son around the world, trying to give him the best education, the best life experiences."

5   But what Jordan calls a dream come true is raising serious concerns within the climbing community. His case has already sparked[2] debate in mountaineering blogs and publications about how young is too young to climb. Some worry whether a 13-year-old can fully comprehend the risks he faces on a peak that has already claimed about 200 lives.

6   "He's got his whole life to climb Everest," said Todd Burleson, leader of eight expeditions and founder of a Seattle-based guide company and mountaineering school, Alpine Ascents International. "Being the youngest boy to climb is a fashionable, celebrity-oriented sort of thing. But it's not about [loving] the mountains. It's like trying to get your PhD at 10."

7   Jordan's father, a flight paramedic, and stepmother, a personal trainer, have no previous experience on Everest. Both are adventure racers, however. The trio has climbed several major peaks, including Kilimanjaro when Jordan was 9. The highest was Aconcagua in Argentina, which stands at about 7,000 metres.

8   For Everest, they have trained with hypoxic altitude tents[3] and hired Sherpas to accompany them to the 8,848-metre high peak on the border of China and Nepal. Mr. Romero has said he's confident in his decision to avoid the $65,000 (U.S.) fee for a professional guide. "We know when to step back, we know when to turn around," he told CNN.

9   But Mr. Burleson warns that Everest is unpredictable. Extreme heights and quickly changing weather can leave climbers vulnerable to frostbite, altitude sickness and death. "Let me tell you: The Himalayas are a whole other world," he said.

---

[1] **unorthodox:** unusual, not typical or traditional
[2] **sparked:** started, as with a first
[3] **hypoxic altitude tent:** a special tent used to train people to tolerate low oxygen levels at high altitudes

10 The Romeros have also made the unusual decision to take the northern route on the Chinese side of the mountain, he said. While the north side has cheaper permit fees and offers more challenges, it also has fewer supports, such as the medical tent on the southern Nepalese side, where Mr. Burleson and other long-term guide companies operate. Generally, the north side attracts budget outfitters[4] with less experience, he said.

11 Comparing the two routes is like comparing "New York City to some wilderness area in Alaska," he said.

12 Even if he makes it up and down part of the mountain safely, leading experts say Jordan risks long-term brain damage.

13 Recent Spanish research found that extreme expeditions left climbers with permanent damage to the frontal lobe, an area that helps people plan, focus and make complex decisions.

14 The part of the brain is still developing in 13-year-olds, said Doug Fields, a developmental neurobiologist and senior researcher with the U.S. National Institutes of Health, who wrote about this topic in Outside Magazine last year.

15 "These were MRIs[5] showing structural damage and it was permanent," Dr. Fields said. "Many high-altitude climbers come back impaired. They get spacey, have trouble focusing."

16 Mr. Romero has pointed out that there's no scientific proof that growing brains are harmed by extreme elevations. That's true, Dr. Fields says, but adds that scientists haven't yet studied young children. Only a handful of teens have reached Everest's summit in recent years —including two 17-year-old American boys and a 15-year-old Nepalese girl.

17 There are two competing theories about the effects of Everest-related hypoxia[6] on growing brains, says Peter Hackett, an emergency physician in Colorado and one of the leading authorities on altitude sickness. "One school of thought is that the not-fully mature brain is more resilient and thus better able to cope with hypoxic stress," he said in an e-mail from Nepal. "Another is that the immature brain is more vulnerable because all connections are not yet formed."

18 Despite the criticism they face, the Romeros say they're happy with their decision to facilitate their son's dream. At 9, Jordan saw a picture of the seven peaks at his school in Big Bear, Calif., and decided he wanted to climb them all. After Everest, the only peak he has left is Vinson Massif in Antarctica; a trip is planned for December.

19 "Yes, I do feel a bit overwhelmed," he told a reporter earlier this week. "I do respect the boundaries and dangers of the mountain. But we're taking all the precautions. We're being as safe as we can. I think we're doing it for all the right reasons."

---

[4] **outfitter**: a company that sells equipment and supplies services for the pursuit of certain activities, in this case mountain climbing
[5] **MRI (magnetic resonance imaging)**: a process used to look inside a body for medical purposes
[6] **hypoxia**: a condition in which a person does not have enough oxygen

The Seven Summits
These are mountains Jordan Romero has climbed.

Date	Peak	Country	Continent	Elevation	
Apr 2006	Kilimanjaro	Tanzania	Africa	5,892 m	19,340 ft
Jul 2007	Elbrus	Russia	Europe	5,642 m	18,510 ft
Dec 2007	Aconcagua	Argentina	South America	6,962 m	22,841 ft
Jun 2008	McKinley (Denali)	Alaska, USA	North America	6,194 m	20,320 ft
Sep 2009	Carstensz Pyramid	Indonesia	Oceania	4,884 m	16.024 ft
May 2010	Everest	China/Nepal	Asia	8,848 m	29,035 ft
Planned	Vinson Massif	—	Antarctica	4,897 m	16,066 ft

Source: "At 13, is Jordan Romero too young to climb Mount Everest?" adapted from "At 13, is Jordan Romero too young to climb Mount Everest?" by Hayley Mick, GLOBE AND MAIL, April 29, 2010. Copyright CTVglobemedia Publishing Inc. All Rights Reserved. Reprinted by permsission.

Building Word Knowledge

Using Word Forms. Many English words have a variety of forms, including verb (v.), noun (n.), adjective (adj.), and adverb (adv.) forms. When you write, be sure to use the correct form of each word.

Look at the chart below. Find the words and their different forms in the reading on page 28. Circle them and notice how they are used. Add the words you find to the chart. Also fill in other forms of these words that you may know. There is no form for the shaded areas.

Verb	Noun	Adjective	Adverb
climb			
		young	
	risk		
			recently
			safely
		mature	
		responsible	

Focused Practice

A. *Read the article again. With a partner, write T (true) or F (false). Discuss the reasons for your answers and correct any false statements. Write the number of the paragraph where the information for each statement is found.*

Paragraph(s)

_____ **1.** Paul Romero sees himself as a good father.   _____

_____ **2.** Todd Burleson thinks Jordan should wait a few years to climb Everest.   _____

_____ **3.** Paul Romero hired a professional guide to lead the expedition up Everest.   _____

_____ **4.** Climbers risk frostbite, altitude sickness, brain damage and even death.   _____

_____ **5.** Taking the north side of Everest is riskier than taking the southern side.

_____ **6.** Many teens have reached the top of Everest.

B. *Read Paul Romero's statement. Do you agree or disagree? Discuss your opinion with a partner.*

"I think it's pretty responsible parenting. I'm taking my son around the world, trying to give him the best education, the best life experiences." —Paul Romero

C. *Read the* Tip for Writers. *Then answer the question in five or six complete sentences Think about your audience as you write.*

Do you think it is a good idea to let a 13-year-old climb one of the highest mountains in the world?

D. *Discuss your answer with a partner. What did you write to help your reader understand the situation and convince him or her of your point of view?*

Growing Up Too Fast? **31**

Writing a Persuasive Essay

An essay is a group of paragraphs about one topic. It is similar to a paragraph in many ways, but it is longer and more developed. An essay usually has an introductory paragraph, one or more body paragraphs, and a concluding paragraph.

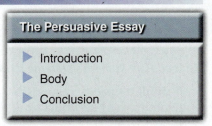

The Persuasive Essay

▶ Introduction
▶ Body
▶ Conclusion

You are going to write a persuasive essay that tries to convince people to share your point of view about an issue. You will write a four-paragraph essay that provides a clearly stated opinion on an issue and a well-organized convincing argument that supports your opinion.

Like a persuasive paragraph, a persuasive essay contains three parts. The chart below compares the structure of a persuasive paragraph and a persuasive essay. Note the similarities between the two.

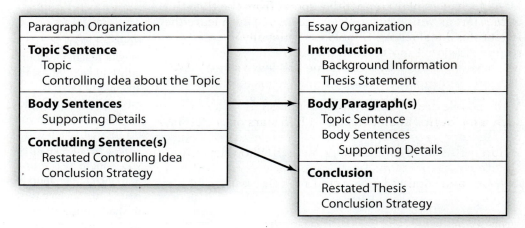

Paragraph Organization	Essay Organization

Topic Sentence
  Topic
  Controlling Idea about the Topic
	Introduction
	  Background Information
	  Thesis Statement

Body Sentences
  Supporting Details
	Body Paragraph(s)
	  Topic Sentence
	  Body Sentences
	    Supporting Details

Concluding Sentence(s)
  Restated Controlling Idea
  Conclusion Strategy
	Conclusion
	  Restated Thesis
	  Conclusion Strategy

The *thesis statement* in an essay is like the *topic sentence* in a paragraph. The thesis states the topic and controlling idea of the whole essay.

The *body paragraphs* are the middle paragraphs of an essay. They divide the supporting ideas of the essay into separate paragraphs. Like a single paragraph, a body paragraph usually begins with a *topic sentence* that states the controlling idea of the paragraph. Both a single paragraph and a body paragraph in an essay contain supporting details to explain the topic sentence.

The *concluding paragraph* in an essay is like the *concluding sentence(s)* in a paragraph. It includes a restatement of the essay's controlling idea and a concluding strategy that ends the essay in an interesting way.

For a persuasive essay, the first step is to select a topic that people have different opinions about. The prewriting step also includes considering various opinions and arguments about the topic before deciding on your opinion. As you decide on your own view or belief, be sure to consider the opposite points of view as well. It is important to think about why people might disagree with your argument.

Your Own Writing

Choosing Your Assignment

A. *Choose Assignment 1 or Assignment 2.*

1. Many teenagers play competitive sports from the time they are young children. Some start as young as five years old. Some even leave their homes and schools to join professional teams. Should exceptionally talented young athletes be allowed to play professional sports when they are still in their early teens even if it means they will have to move away from home and leave school? Write a persuasive essay that develops and supports your opinion on this issue.

2. Many people dream of becoming famous television or movie actors, and sometimes such fame begins at an early age. Child stars often get their education through private tutoring and have only limited opportunities for social interaction with other children outside of the acting profession. Should parents encourage their young children to become famous movie or television stars? Write a persuasive essay that develops and supports your opinion on this issue.

B. *Freewrite for ten minutes on your assignment. Here are some questions to get you started:*

- Why did you choose this assignment?

- What kind of life do you think a young person would have in an adult professional world? What would be some of the benefits? What would be some of the drawbacks?

- Have you ever known or heard about someone who had to make a similar choice?

- Why might someone disagree with your point of view?

- What more do you want to find out?

C. Checking in. *Work with a partner who chose the same assignment. Discuss the ideas and details you wrote in Exercise B. Ask your partner some questions about his or her topic. Did your partner . . .*

- express an opinion about what life would be like for a young person in a professional world?

- talk about benefits and drawbacks?

- consider other people's points of view?

Share your point of view about your partner's topic. Based on your discussion, make changes and additions to your writing. ➡

D. *Complete the T-chart. List the benefits and drawbacks of letting young people enter the professional world. Focus only on the assignment you chose on page 33. Try to fill in at least three points on both sides of the issue. You will have a chance to review, change, or add information later in the unit.*

Benefits (advantages)	Drawbacks (disadvantages)
to improve your talent	Dangerous environment
to save money	

■ THE INTRODUCTION

The *introductory paragraph* of an academic essay contains two parts:

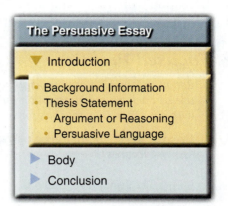

1. *Background information* about the topic of the essay helps your reader understand and become interested in the topic. Before you begin writing, ask yourself: *What important background information does my reader need to know?* or *What's the situation that I am writing about?* Do not give too many details—provide only what the reader needs.

2. The *thesis statement* presents the controlling idea of the essay. It may be one or two sentences. In a persuasive essay, your thesis statement will include your opinion or point of view on the issue. The thesis statement is typically the last sentence of the introductory paragraph.

In a persuasive essay, the background often includes opposing views people have about the issue. Then the thesis statement presents the writer's opinion or point of view. The thesis statement in a persuasive essay is similar to the topic sentence in a persuasive paragraph because you want to convince your reader to share your point of view. Therefore, your thesis statement should also have *persuasive language*—words and phrases that suggest that you are giving an opinion. You learned about some of these words and phrases in Unit 1. Other examples of persuasive language include:

I strongly believe that . . .   *It is a mistake to . . .*
It is irresponsible to . . .   *It is definitely the right decision to . . .*
It is a good idea to . . .

Example:

background
↓

[Children are full of energy and ideas; however, their ideas don't always make sense. Sometimes their ideas might even be dangerous. The role of parents is to guide their children and, when necessary, to make proper decisions for their protection. This can be tricky. On the one hand, parents don't want to put their child in harm's way, but on the other hand, they don't want to step on their child's dreams either. Paul Romero faced such a challenge when his nine-year-old son, Jordan, expressed a desire to climb the Seven Summits, the highest peaks on each of the seven continents. I can appreciate his desire to educate his son and

thesis statement

help Jordan pursue his dreams.] [However, I strongly believe that Paul Romero's decision to allow Jordan to climb these mountains was foolish and irresponsible.]

| persuasive language | issue | opinion |

Growing Up Too Fast?   **35**

Notice that the background information in the example gives some details about the topic and then briefly presents different perspectives on the issue. The writer also provides basic information about Paul and Jordan Romero, and expresses an understanding of why Paul Romero made the choice he did. Then in the thesis statement, the writer uses the transition word *however* and persuasive language to express his contrasting point of view, which he will develop and support in the rest of the essay.

Focused Practice

A. *Read the following essay assignment and the sentences. Check (✓) the details that you might use as background information for an introductory paragraph on this topic. Discuss your answers with a partner. Give reasons for your choices when you and your partner have different opinions.*

Do you agree or disagree with the decision to let a thirteen-year-old climb Mount Everest?

_____ **1.** Jordan Romero is 13 years old.

_____ **2.** Jordan Romero is from California.

_____ **3.** The decision to let Jordan Romero climb Mount Everest is very controversial.

_____ **4.** Mount Everest is the tallest peak in the world.

_____ **5.** Jordan Romero studies algebra.

_____ **6.** It was Jordan's dream to climb the seven tallest summits in the world.

_____ **7.** Mountain climbing is a dangerous sport.

_____ **8.** Jordan wants to climb Mount Vinson Massif in Antarctica next.

B. *Review the essay assignment in Exercise A and read the sentences below. Check (✓) the sentences that would make a good thesis statement for an essay on this topic. Discuss your answers with a partner. Give reasons for your choices when you and your partner have different opinions.*

_____ **1.** Therefore, I think it is a mistake to let such a young boy make such a dangerous climb.

_____ **2.** In my opinion, a 13-year-old is too young to take such a risk.

_____ **3.** I agree with Paul Romero.

_____ **4.** If I were his parent, I would not allow him to climb Mount Everest.

_____ **5.** A 13-year-old should focus on other things.

_____ **6.** If we examine the specifics of this case, it is clear that the decision to allow Jordan Romero to climb Mount Everest was the right one.

_____ **7.** Jordan Romero's father made the right decision to allow his son to follow his dreams and pursue his passion.

_____ **8.** I wish I could have climbed up Mount Everest with Jordan and his group.

C. *Review the essay assignment in Exercise A and this model of an introductory paragraph. Then answer the questions with a partner.*

When you meet Jordan Romero, he may seem to be an ordinary 13-year-old boy, but his goals and passions are anything but ordinary. One day when he was just nine years old, Jordan saw a picture of the Seven Summits, the highest mountains in the world, and told his father, Paul, that he wanted to climb them all. Wanting to encourage his son and give him the best education possible, Paul Romero began working hard to help make his son's dream come true. He has arranged for Jordan to climb many of the highest peaks in the world, including Mount Everest, the highest. Some may see Paul Romero as the perfect father. However, I strongly disagree. Regardless of the boy's desire to climb Mount Everest, it was irresponsible for the adults in his life to let him make such a dangerous climb.

1. Which information from Exercise A did the writer include as background? Write the numbers of the statements here: __1/4/6/1/7__

2. Where does the writer present the other side of the issue? Underline the sentence(s) that express a point of view that is different from the writer's.

3. What opinion does the thesis statement express? Circle the words the writer uses to express his opinion.

Your Own Writing

Finding Out More

A. *You may want to learn more about the topic you chose on page 33.*

- If you chose Assignment 1, online or at the library, find out more about young athletes. Look for information about the careers of athletes who turned pro when they were still in their teens. Find out more about specific athletes who chose not to turn pro at a young age. When you search for information online, use keywords such as *child athlete* or *turning pro*, and names such as Monica Selles, Freddy Adu, and Michelle Wie.

- If you chose Assignment 2, online or at the library, find out more about young movie and TV actors. Look for information about TV or movie actors who began their careers when they were young children. When you search for information online, use keywords such as *child stars* or *child TV stars*, and names such as Shirley Temple, Gary Coleman, and Drew Barrymore.

B. *Take notes about what you found out. Add new arguments for or against your topic to your T-chart on page 34. Write down specific information about any challenges, rewards, and possible regrets these people experienced as a result of entering the professional world at a young age.*

C. Checking in. *Share your information with your partner. Did your partner . . .*

- find enough information about the topic?

- choose relevant examples for the topic?

- find reasons why people would have an opposing point of view?

- use at least three reliable sources?

Use this information when you write your essay.

Planning Your Introduction

A. *List the background information you will need to include in your introduction. Be sure to include information about an opposing point of view.*

_____

_____

_____

_____

B. *Write a draft of your thesis statement. Make sure your thesis statement clearly presents your opinion. Look back at your freewriting and your T-chart to help you.*

_____

_____

C. Checking in. *Share your thesis statement with a partner. Did your partner . . .*

- clearly state the topic and express an opinion about it?

- include persuasive language to make the argument clear and convincing?

Tell your partner what you like about his or her thesis statement. If you have any suggestions for improving it, share them. Then tell your partner what kind of supporting evidence you expect to see in his or her essay, based on the thesis statement.

D. *Based on your partner's feedback, you may want to rewrite your thesis statement.*

■ THE BODY

The *body paragraphs* of an essay develop and support the point of view that is expressed in the thesis statement. Just as a paragraph has a group of sentences that support the topic sentence, an essay contains one or more paragraphs that provide information in support of the thesis statement.

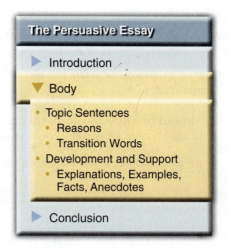

Writing Topic Sentences

In an essay, each body paragraph usually begins with a *topic sentence*. These sentences often rephrase and build on the thesis statement. In a persuasive essay, your topic sentences should mention the topic and the controlling idea. They might also include your point of view or opinion. Your topic sentences should include one specific reason that supports the opinion you expressed in your thesis statement. Then the rest of the body paragraph develops and supports that reason with more information, such as explanations, examples, facts, and anecdotes—brief stories from your own experience.

To connect your ideas from paragraph to paragraph, it is important to use transition words. In a persuasive essay, listing order transition words in topic sentences helps your reader to follow your argument. These transition words can be placed in two different groups.

Group 1: Often Used with *Because*	Group 2: Often Used with *Reason*
First,	One reason
Second,	The second reason
Additionally,	Another reason
Most important,	The most important reason
Finally,	The final reason

Notice that the transition words in Group 1 are followed by a comma. The transition words in Group 2 are often used in a three-part sentence with *that . . . is that*.

Examples:

First, teenagers like Jordan Romero should not be allowed to make such dangerous climbs **because** young people need a stable home environment.

One reason **that** teenagers like Jordan Romero should not be allowed to make such dangerous climbs **is that** young people need a stable home environment.

Focused Practice

A. *Read the following essay assignment. Then combine each set of sentences below into two different topic sentences for a body paragraph, using the transition words. The first one is done for you.*

Do you agree or disagree with the decision to let Jordan Romero climb the Seven Summits?

1. Jordan should be encouraged to take these risks.
He could make a lot of money for himself and his family.

First, *Jordan Romero should be encouraged to take these risks because he could make a lot of money for himself and his family.*

The first reason *that Jordan should be encouraged to take these risks is that he could make a lot of money for himself and his family.*

2. I think letting him climb Everest was a mistake.
Mother Nature is too unpredictable.

Another reason *I think letting him climb was a mistake is because Mother Nature is too unpredictable.*

Additionally, *letting him climb to the top of Everest has a mistake because Mother Nature is too unpredictable.*

3. I think his father made the right decision.
This is because it is a unique opportunity for Jordan to see the world.

Most important, *I think his father made the right decision because it is a unique opportunity...*

The most important reason *is that it is a unique opportunity for Jordan to see the world.*

4. I disagree with the decision to let Jordan climb.
He is not mature enough to make important decisions.

Finally, _____

_____

The final reason _____

_____

5. I disagree with the decision.
   Jordan is simply too young to have such a dangerous hobby.

   More important, _____

   _____

   Another important reason _____

   _____

6. I agree with the decision to allow him to climb Everest.
   It is his dream to do so, and parents should help their children pursue their dreams.

   Second, _____

   _____

   The second reason _____

   _____

B. *Review the essay assignment in Exercise A and the following thesis statement. Write a topic sentence for the first body paragraph of the essay. Make sure that your topic sentence includes the issue, your point of view/opinion, and a transition. Compare your topic sentence with a partner's. Then discuss how the sentence might change if it were the topic sentence for the second body paragraph in this essay. Write it below.*

Thesis Statement: It was definitely the right decision to allow 13-year-old Jordan Romero to climb the Seven Summits.

_____

_____ Each one of the Seven Summits is
different. They are on different continents, so he will learn about those continents.
He will meet people from countries nearby and learn about their culture and
customs. He might even become interested in their languages. For example, when
he climbed Everest, he was in China. He likely met Chinese or Nepalese people
and learned to communicate with them. He probably learned about their lives,
their families, and their food. The lives of the Sherpas are surely very different
from his own. Climbing the Seven Summits is a valuable experience and Jordan is
fortunate that his father made it happen for him.

Topic sentence for the second body paragraph: _____

_____

Developing a Body Paragraph

When you wrote a persuasive paragraph in Unit 1, you learned about supporting an opinion with reasons, examples, facts, and anecdotes. In a persuasive essay, the topic sentences of your body paragraphs will state the reasons for your opinion and you will develop and support those reasons with supporting details such as explanations, examples, facts, or anecdotes.

Examples:

Fact: Each of the Seven Summits is on a different continent.

Explanation: Because these summits are on different continents, Jordan will be able to learn about the people, customs, and culture in different parts of the world.

Example: For example, when he was in China, he probably learned things about the Chinese language, families, and food.

Fact: Jordan was nine years old when he first learned about the Seven Summits.

Explanation: Wanting to encourage his son and give him the best education possible, Paul Romero began working hard to help make his son's dream come true. He must have believed that these experiences would have a lasting effect on Jordan and his future.

Anecdote: When I was a teen, my family lived in Nepal. I became interested in the art of Nepalese wood carving and its connection to architecture. My experiences there have greatly influenced my decisions about my education and career.

Some writers choose to end a body paragraph with an interesting or thought-provoking comment or question. Others return to the controlling idea in the topic sentence and sum up the reason. You might also choose to wait until the concluding paragraph to summarize your reasoning and argument.

Examples:

Summary: Climbing the Seven Summits is a valuable experience, and Jordan is fortunate that his father made it happen for him.

Thought-Provoking Question: What better way is there for a teenager to learn about the world?

Focused Practice

A. *Read this paragraph. Then check (✓) the ways in which the writer supports the controlling idea in the topic sentence. Discuss your answers with a partner.*

> Secondly, this was the right decision because it is a unique opportunity for
> Jordan to spend quality time with his father and stepmother. These days it is rare
> for parents and children to be together and do things as a family. In most families
> the parents go to work in the morning and the children go to school. After school,
> family members all have their own activities—shopping, meetings, clubs, and
> sports. Many teens just waste time hanging out with their friends. Some families
> might have dinner together or do things together on the weekends, but even this is
>
> *(continued)*

becoming increasingly rare. Teenagers want their independence. Often, they don't even want to be seen by their friends in public with their parents. That's the way I was when I was a teen. I didn't hate my parents, but it wasn't "cool" to be seen with them. However, the Romeros are clearly different. Not only are they seen in public together, but they also spend months at a time together. More important, they are building a strong connection and memories that they will share and value for the rest of their lives. We shouldn't criticize them. We should be jealous.

_____ The writer explains what *unique opportunity* means.

_____ The writer gives examples of what he means by *quality time*.

_____ The writer explains why quality time is an issue.

_____ The writer explains why he thinks it's rare for parents and children to spend time together.

_____ The writer gives examples of the types of memories the Romeros will share.

_____ The writer explains how the Romeros are different from other families.

_____ The writer provides an anecdote.

B. *Work with a partner. Read the thesis statement and two body paragraphs. Then fill in the examples that best complete each paragraph. One sentence does not fit.*

Thesis Statement: Allowing his son to climb Mount Everest was probably the smartest decision Paul Romero will ever make.

The first reason that it was a smart idea for Jordan to climb Everest is that he could become rich and famous. The Romeros could take advantage of people's interest in their family's adventures. _____ 2

_____ make money and fame _____

Jordan's father is a model for how all parents should encourage their children

(continued)

to work hard and achieve their goals. Paul Romero could write about being a successful, although unorthodox, parent. With these books and the speaking tours, Jordan and his father will never have to work again. Furthermore, they could also endorse sporting goods, like mountain climbing equipment and clothing. _then_

5 _they have Knowlegde un this enviroment_

These business ventures would give them a rewarding and comfortable future. Paul Romero should be praised for giving his son such a promising future.

Another reason why I think this was a smart decision is that people should follow their dreams while they are young. _Because he have_

3 _talent and time to use your abilities_

We go to college or get a job. Many people get married and have a family. Most people work hard every day just to make ends meet. These daily responsibilities or obligations often cause people to lose sight of their dreams, which is sad. _After_

4 _that these people to give up your dreams_

Does it dry up like a raisin in the sun? Does it smell like rotten meat? Does it explode? Hughes is suggesting that it is a tragedy to ignore a dream. It is the same for Jordan. _the enjoy your opportunity with_

6 _your family and_

These people should congratulate Jordan on fulfilling his dreams and, instead, work on fulfilling their own.

1. Sports stars like Michael Jordan and Tiger Woods have made millions of dollars from endorsing Nike products.

2. From the time he was nine years old, Jordan Romero's dream was crystal clear.

3. In his poem "A Dream Deferred," Langston Hughes wonders about all of the unfortunate things that might happen to a dream if we do not pursue it.

4. As we get older, the challenges of daily life get greater and greater.

5. For example, Jordan and his father could write a book about how to climb dangerous mountains or about how to face difficult challenges without giving up.

6. Perhaps people who disagree with the decision to let Jordan climb are just jealous or frustrated because they cannot pursue their own deferred dreams.

C. *Read the following body paragraph. Then fill in the sentence that best concludes the paragraph. Discuss your answer with a partner.*

> Their poor planning is one reason that I think it was a mistake to let this boy climb Everest. To reach the top safely, a climber or a team of climbers must have a carefully designed plan. The Romeros didn't have one. First, Paul Romero did not hire a professional guide to lead the expedition. This decision was reckless. Romero and his wife are not trained guides, and Mount Everest is the highest mountain in the world. According to the article "At 13, is Jordan Romero too young to climb Mount Everest?", more than 200 people have died trying to reach the summit. Furthermore, the article also reports that the Romeros chose to go up the Chinese side of the mountain, which is cheaper but more challenging. These two choices made a dangerous trip even more dangerous. _____
>
> _____
>
> _____

1. In addition, medical facilities are not available on the Chinese side, so climbers do not have as much support.

2. Paul Romero should be ashamed of himself for putting his son and the other climbers at such great risk.

3. Without a plan, the Romeros were taking unnecessary chances, and Paul Romero was placing his son, his wife, and himself in tremendous danger.

4. Finally, the weather on Mt. Everest is extremely unpredictable.

Your Own Writing

Planning Your Body Paragraphs

A. *Before you begin writing your body paragraphs, complete the outline below. Copy your thesis statement from page 38.*

- Write a topic sentence and supporting details for each of your body paragraphs.

- If you want to include a concluding sentence, write one for each body paragraph.

Persuasive Essay

▶ Thesis Statement: _How young us too yong for an Iphone_

10 years old

▶ Body Paragraph 1

    ▶ Topic Sentence: _Iphone_

        ▶ Supporting Details:

- _the children loe consontration_

- _children expose a unmesurel unformation_

        ▶ Concluding Sentence (Optional): _the parents need put climited for use Iphone._

▶ Body Paragraph 2

    ▶ Topic Sentence: _Before age of 10 children need other interest_

        ▶ Supporting Details:

- _play with other children_

- _play sports_

- _play music and reads books_

        ▶ Concluding Sentence (Optional): _Children need enjoy your childhood leke chils_

B. Checking in. *Share your outline with a partner. Did your partner . . .*

- provide interesting reasons to support the thesis statement?

- provide supporting facts, explanations, examples, or anecdotes that are relevant and interesting?

C. *Based on your partner's feedback, you may want to rewrite parts of your outline.*

■ THE CONCLUSION

Just as a *paragraph* ends with a *concluding sentence*, an *essay* ends with a *concluding paragraph* that returns to the idea in the thesis statement.

In the concluding paragraph, restate the opinion expressed in the thesis statement using different words. Then use a concluding strategy to persuade the reader that the point of view expressed is valid. In the case of an essay about Paul Romero's decision to let Jordan climb Mt. Everest, for example, you would say whether or not you agree with that decision and restate why. Then you might return to the opposing point of view you mentioned in your introduction and point out why your point of view is better.

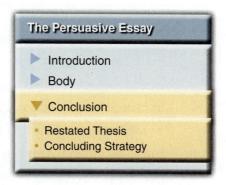

Your conclusion does not need to be very long—just long enough to return to the controlling idea in your thesis statement and end in an interesting and persuasive way.

To signal to your reader that you are concluding your essay, you may also want to use a transition word or phrase such as *In conclusion . . .* to begin your conclusion. However, if you return to the controlling idea in your thesis statement in a clear way, a transition word or phrase may not always be necessary.

To conclude your essay in an interesting, convincing way, use one or more of these strategies:

1. Look to the future of the issue and comment on it.

2. Propose an alternative that should have or could have been done and explain what might have happened as a result.

3. Summarize the opposing point of view that you mentioned in your introduction and show again why your point of view is better.

Focused Practice

Read these concluding paragraphs and answer the questions.

1.

> In conclusion, the decision to allow this boy to climb Mount Everest and the other dangerous mountains was a mistake. Like any young teen, he is not physically and mentally prepared to take on such a challenge. He should have waited until he was several years older. Instead of teaching Jordan about "instant gratification," his father could have given him a valuable lesson in "delayed gratification." If Jordan had waited, he could have learned even more about the Seven Summits. An older and wiser Jordan would have been able to independently decide what he wanted to do and to be truly proud of his own choices and accomplishments. It's true that he did climb Mt. Everest. However, he only followed his team up the mountain. As the article stated, he was just a "passenger." If he had waited a little longer he might have been able to say that he had planned and accomplished it himself.

2.

> It is understandable how people might think that letting Jordan Romero climb Everest at such a young age was a mistake; however, if you look at the positive effects, it is clear that the benefits outweigh the drawbacks. Jordan is on track for an incredible future. Not only will he have excitement during his teen years, but he will also learn a lot and be able to make a lot of money. He may also build a successful career as a result of these early adventures. He may only be 13, but he has his whole life ahead of him to look forward to.

1. What is the writer's restated thesis in each paragraph? Circle the sentence(s).

2. Which strategy or strategies did each writer use to close the essay?

Paragraph 1: _____

Paragraph 2: _____

Your Own Writing

Planning Your Conclusion

A. *How will you rephrase your thesis statement in the conclusion? List your ideas here.*

_____

_____

B. *What strategy will you use to close the essay?*

_____

_____

C. Checking in. *Share your ideas with a partner. Did your partner . . .*

- discover a new and interesting way to return to the thesis statement?
- choose an effective concluding strategy?

Writing Your First Draft

Read the Tip for Writers. *Review your notes on pages 34, 38, and 46. Then write the first draft of your essay. When you are finished, give your essay a working title. Hand in your draft to your teacher.*

Tip for Writers
When you write your first draft, be sure that you have considered your **intended audience** and thought about the opinions they might have about the issue.

Revising your work is an essential part of the writing process. This is your opportunity to be sure that your essay has all the important pieces and that it is clear.

u'noy

Focused Practice

A. *You have read parts of this persuasive essay already. Now read the entire essay to see how the parts fit together.*

A Parent's Job Is to Protect

Children are full of energy and ideas; however, their ideas don't always make sense. Sometimes their ideas might even be dangerous. The role of parents is to guide their children and, when necessary, to make proper decisions for their protection. This can be tricky. On the one hand, parents don't want to put their child in harm's way, but on the other hand, they don't want to step on their child's dreams either. Paul Romero faced such a challenge when his nine-year-old son, Jordan, expressed a desire to climb the Seven Summits, the highest peaks on each of the seven continents. I can appreciate his desire to educate his son and help Jordan pursue his dreams. However, I strongly believe that Paul Romero's decision to allow Jordan to climb these mountains, and especially Mt. Everest, was foolish and irresponsible.

First of all, his family should not have let him climb because he is physically too young to do it. Even though at 5'8" and 140 pounds, he is above average for a 13-year-old boy, his body is still growing. His bones and muscles are still growing and his brain is still developing. Researchers are not sure about the effect of high altitudes on teenagers because they have not studied teens specifically. Some say it can cause long-term brain damage. The article, "At 13, is Jordan Romero too young to climb Mount Everest?" quotes a leading authority on altitude sickness, Peter Hackett. He said that some researchers believe that a young brain is more resilient than an adult brain, but others argue that the brains of the young are more vulnerable. Clearly the research is not conclusive. However, I don't understand why a parent would put a growing child at risk in this way.

Another reason why I think the decision was wrong is that Mother Nature is too unpredictable. We have seen the destructive potential of storms such as Hurricane Katrina in New Orleans, Louisiana. Even specialists could not handle or control the effects of that storm. How will a 13-year-old make the tough decisions

(continued)

---

he needs to when faced with the destructive power of nature? If he makes one mistake, he could affect the lives of those traveling with him. Look at the case of Abby Sunderland, the 13-year-old girl who was encouraged by her father to sail solo around the world. In the end the weather conditions were just too challenging for her to handle. She and her boat were lost at sea. Only after a desperate and expensive search was Abby found and brought home to safety. The event was too much for her and she had to be rescued. Granted, Jordan Romero was not climbing alone, but the natural dangers of Everest were still there. It's a parent's responsibility to protect children—not to put them in harm's way. Why would parents even be willing to let their child be in such a dangerous situation?

I believe that any responsible parent would disapprove of the decision to allow a boy to climb such a dangerous mountain at such a young age. Supporters of Paul Romero point to the fact that this climb was successful. They reached the summit and no one was seriously hurt along the way. However, what will happen next time? Jordan Romero's climb sends the wrong message to kids and parents. I hope that other families will avoid taking such risks. It's great to get an education through experience and to follow one's dreams, but not with the costs of risking good health or life itself.

B. *Work with a partner. Answer the questions about the essay.*

1. Which sentences give background information about the topic? Label them *background*.

2. Where does the writer refer to the opposing point of view? Circle it.

3. What is the thesis statement? Underline it.

4. What transition words does the writer use to introduce the topic sentences of the body paragraphs? Circle them.

5. What evidence does the writer give to support and develop the controlling idea in each body paragraph? Double underline the evidence in each body paragraph.

6. What is the restated thesis? Underline it.

7. Which concluding strategy does the writer use?

C. Checking in. *Discuss your marked-up essay with another pair of students. Then in your group, share one thing about the essay that you found the most interesting. Explain your answer.*

Building Word Knowledge

Using Word Forms. The writer of "A Parent's Job Is to Protect" used forms of the words that appear in the chart below.

A. *Find and circle these words and their other forms. Notice how they are used. Add other forms to the chart.*

Verb	Noun	Adjective	Adverb
	dangers	*dangerous*	*dangerously*
challenge	*Challenge*	*challenging*	
protect	*protection*	*unpredictable*	
	responsibility	*responsible to*	*responsibility*
unresponsibility	irresponsible		

B. *Complete each sentence with the correct word.*

1. **dangerous, dangerously, dangers**

   a. Some parents choose to live ___*dangerously*___, but they shouldn't allow their children to do so.

   b. Most people don't realize just how ___*dangers*___ it is to climb Mount Everest.

   c. Experienced climbers are more likely to be aware of the mountain's hidden ___*dangers*___.

2. **challenge, challenging, challenges**

   a. Doing homework at home can be hard, but doing it on a mountain can present even greater ___*challenges*___.

   b. Heather's teammates ___*challenging*___ her to be a better player every day.

   c. Mountain climbing is a ___*challenge*___ sport.

3. **protect, protected, protection**

   a. On a mountain climb, there is often little ___*protection*___ from the weather.

   b. The adults in Jordan Romero's life ___*protect*___ him from harm.

   c. He doesn't seem worried at all. I'm sure he feels very ___*protected*___.

(continued)

4. responsibility, responsible, responsibly

a. If Jordan does not act _responsibly_, he could put other people's lives in danger.

b. It was really Jordan's _responsibility_ to make sure his school work was finished.

c. If anything happens to a young person working in an adult profession, it is the

child's parents who are _responsible_ for the child's safety.

C. *Review the draft of your essay. Notice if you have used any of these words. Circle the words in your essay. Then choose three more words from the chart and use each one in a sentence about your topic. You may want to use these sentences in your essay.*

1. _____

2. _____

3. _____

Your Own Writing

Revising Your Draft

A. *Reread the first draft of your essay. Use the Revision Checklist to identify parts of your writing that might need improvement.*

B. *Review your plans and notes and your responses to the Revision Checklist. Then revise your first draft. Save your revised essay. You will look at it again in the next section.*

Revision Checklist

Did you . . .

☐ express the controlling idea of the whole essay in your thesis statement?

☐ give enough essential background in your introduction?

☐ present an opposing point of view in your introduction?

☐ introduce your topic sentences with transition words?

☐ give enough explanations, facts, examples, or anecdotes to develop and support your controlling ideas?

☐ restate the controlling idea of the essay in your conclusion?

☐ use an effective concluding strategy?

☐ use a variety of word forms correctly?

☐ give your essay an interesting title?

■ GRAMMAR PRESENTATION

Before you hand in your revised essay, you must check it for any errors in grammar, punctuation, and spelling. In this section you will learn about the verbs *make*, *have*, *let*, *help*, and *get*. You will focus on this grammar when you edit and proofread your essay.

Make, Have, Let, Help, and *Get*

Grammar Notes	Examples
1. Use *make*, *have* and *get* to talk about things that one person causes another person to do. These verbs show how much choice the other person has about doing the action	
a. *make* + object + base form of the verb often means to force a person to do something. There is no choice.	• His parents didn't **make** *him* **climb** Everest. He wanted to do it.
b. *have* + object + base form of the verb often means to cause a person to do a task. There is some choice.	• The climbers didn't carry their luggage and supplies. They **had** *the porters* **carry** them.
c. *get* + object + infinitive often means to persuade a person to do something by giving rewards or good reasons. There is a choice.	• Paul Romero **got** *his son* **to do** his algebra homework by threatening to cancel the climb up Everest.
BE CAREFUL! *Get* is always followed by **object + infinitive**, NOT the base form of the verb.	Not: Team Romero got Sherpas ~~carry~~ their luggage and supplies.
Make can also mean to have an effect on something or someone.	• The high altitude **made** *the climbers* **feel** sick.
2. *Let* + object + base form of the verb means to allow a person to do something. **BE CAREFUL!** *Allow* is followed by **object + infinitive**, NOT the base form of the verb.	• How can parents **let** *their child* **do** something so dangerous? • How can parents **allow** *their children* **to do** something so dangerous? Not: How can parents allow their children ~~do~~ something so dangerous?
3. *Help* means to make something easier for a person. Help can be followed by: **object + base form of the verb** OR **object + infinitive** The meaning is the same.	• Paul Romero **is helping** *Jordan* **follow** his dreams. OR • Paul Romero **is helping** *Jordan* **to follow** his dreams.

less choice ↑ ↓ *more choice*

Focused Practice

A. *Read the sentences. Complete the sentences with* make, have, let, help, get, *or* allow. *Use the clue in parentheses as a guide.*

1. People debate whether or not it is a good idea to _____ *let* _____ a 13-year-old

   do something so dangerous. *(permit)*

2. It was easy to _____ *get* _____ his father to climb these mountains, too. They

   both love adventure. *(persuade)*

3. Barbara couldn't _____ *get* _____ her teenagers to climb a mountain with her.

   (persuade)

4. Would you _____ *allau* _____ your child to do something so dangerous? *(permit)*

5. I don't think it is a mistake to _____ *let* _____ a young teen climb Everest.

   (permit)

6. During the climb they _____ *have* _____ a volunteer take pictures for Jordan's

   webpage. *(cause)*

7. Schools should not _____ *allau* _____ young people to leave regular schools until

   they are at least 16. *(permit)*

8. Paul Romero is _____ *helping* _____ to make his son's dreams come true. *(assisting)*

9. They didn't _____ *make* _____ him go on these adventures. He chose to go. *(force)*

B. *Read and edit the paragraph. There are six errors in the use of* make, have, let, help *or* get. *The first error has been corrected for you. Find and correct five more.*

> Another reason that I do not think it is a mistake is that it is a unique
> opportunity for him to learn about responsibility. Many people complain that
> Jordan was too young to make life-or-death decisions on these intense climbs.
> However, he has proven that he was up to the challenge. Typically, parents try to get
>   *to*
> their teens take responsibility for things. They let their kids ~~to~~ do chores like taking
>   *to*
> out the garbage or cleaning their bedrooms. Parents also want their kids to study
>   *to*
> hard and be respectful of others even when they don't want to. But it's really hard
>
> *(continued)*

to allow teens ~~to~~ do things they don't want to do. They want independence. They
don't want to be told what to do. At some point parents have to let their teens ~~to~~
have some freedom and allow them taking some responsibility. Gradually, they
will learn to accept the consequences of the choices they make. Paul Romero saw
an opportunity to help his son Jordan learns about taking responsibility. Someone
should give him an award for "Father of the Year."

C. *Write five sentences related to the assignment you chose on page 33. Use causative verbs. These*
may be sentences you already have in your essay.

1. _____

_____

2. _____

_____

3. _____

_____

4. _____

_____

5. _____

_____

Your Own Writing

Editing Your Draft

A. *Use the Editing Checklist to edit and proofread your essay.*

B. *Prepare a clean copy of the final draft of your essay and hand it in to your teacher.*

Editing Checklist

Did you . . .

☐ use *make, have, let, help,* and *get* correctly?

☐ use correct verb forms, punctuation, and spelling?

☐ use the correct forms of words (adjectives, adverbs, verbs, nouns)?

Being Part of the Solution

IN THIS UNIT   You will be writing an essay about a problem at school or in the workplace and a possible solution.

There is a saying, "You can lead a horse to water, but you can't make it drink." The saying expresses a common problem: It is difficult to motivate someone to do something that he or she does not really want to do. Some people believe that the best solution is to offer incentives—money, gifts, or special privileges—that will make people work harder or do something they do not want to do. What do you think is the best way to motivate someone?

Planning for Writing

■ BRAINSTORM

A. *What motivates students to do well in school? Make a list of rewards or incentives that schools or parents offer or could offer to motivate students. Share your list with a partner. Add to your list.*

Motivate class. Supporting with homework.

Pay for private teachers.

_____

B. Using a Problem-Solution Chart. When you write about a problem, you can use a problem-solution chart to describe what the problem is, some of its causes and effects, and how it might be solved.

Work with a partner. Read the problem at the top left side of the chart. Discuss causes and effects of the problem and possible solutions. Then write your ideas in the chart.

What is the problem?
Students in this school are getting low grades.

Why is this a problem? (effects)
1. Students with low grades may not pass their courses.
2. may not get to college.
3. They may fail when it comes to use those information
4.
5. Students with low grades in college may not find a job.

What are some causes of the problem?
- lack of motivation - to not get along with their teachers - they don't like studying.

What are some solutions to the problem?
- Better motivation - private polls - make the class funnier.

Read the magazine article about paying students to do better in school.

TIME

Is Cash the Answer?

By Amanda Ripley   An excerpt from TIME magazine

1   Since there have been children, there have been adults trying to get them to cooperate. Over the centuries, the stick (or paddle or switch) has lost favor, in most cases, to the carrot.[1] Today the petty bribes—a sticker for using the toilet or a cookie for sitting still in church—start before kids can speak in full sentences.

2   In recent years hundreds of schools have made these transactions more businesslike, experimenting with paying kids with cold, hard cash for showing up and getting good grades.

3   I have not met a child who does not admire this trend. But it makes adults profoundly uncomfortable. Teachers complain that we are rewarding kids for doing what they should be doing of their own volition. Psychologists warn that money can actually make kids perform worse by cheapening the act of learning. Parents predict widespread slacking after the incentives go away. And at least one think-tank scholar has denounced the strategy as racist. The debate has become a proxy battle for the larger war over why kids are not learning at the rate they should be despite decades of reforms and budget increases.

4   But all this time, there has been only one real question, particularly in America's lowest performing schools: Does it work? To find out, a Harvard economist named Roland Fryer, Jr. did something education researchers almost never do: he ran a randomized experiment in hundreds of classrooms in multiple cities. He used mostly private money to pay 18,000 kids a total of $6.3 million and brought in a team of researchers to help him analyze the effects. He got death threats, but he carried on. The results, which he shared exclusively with TIME, represent the largest study of financial incentives in the classroom—and one of the more rigorous studies ever on anything in educational policy.

5   The experiment ran in four cities: Chicago, Dallas, Washington, and New York. Each city had its own unique model of incentives, to see which would work best. Some kids were paid for good test scores and others for not fighting with one another. The results are fascinating and surprising. They remind us that kids, like grownups, are not puppets.[2] They don't always respond the way we expect.

6   In the cities where Fryer expected the most success, the experiment had no effect at all—"as zero as zero gets," as he puts it. In two other cities, the results were promising but in totally different ways. In the last city, something remarkable happened. Kids who got paid all year under a very elegant scheme performed significantly better on their standardized reading tests at the end of the year. Statistically speaking, it was as if those kids had spent three extra months in school, compared with their peers who did not get paid.

7   "These are substantial effects, as large as many other interventions that people have thought to be successful," says Brian Jacob, a University of Michigan public-policy and economics professor who has studied the incentives and who reviewed Fryer's study at TIME's request. If incentives are designed wisely, it appears, payments can indeed boost kids' performance as much or more

---

[1] **carrot (-and-stick approach):** a way of making someone do something that combines a promise of good (carrot) if they do it and a threat of something bad (being hit with a stick) if they do not do it

[2] **puppets:** models of people or animals that you can move by pulling wires or strings or by putting your hand inside it

than many other reforms you've heard about before—and for a fraction[3] of the cost.

8   Money is not enough. (It never is.) But for some kids, it may be part of the solution. In the end, we all want our children to grow into self-motivated adults. The question is, How do we help them get there? And is it possible that at least for some kids, the road is paved[4] not with stickers but with $20 bills?

[3] **fraction:** a very small amount of something
[4] **paved (paved the way for something):** covered

	DALLAS	CHICAGO	WASHINGTON	NEW YORK CITY
WHAT STUDENTS WERE PAID FOR	Reading	Grades	Various[†]	Test scores
GRADES PARTICIPATING	Second-graders	Ninth-graders	Sixth-, seventh- and eighth-graders	Fourth- and seventh-graders
HOW MUCH	$2 per book	$50 for A's $35 for B's $20 for C's	Up to $100 every two weeks	$25 (fourth-graders) $50 (seventh-graders) per test
AVERAGE STUDENT EARNED	$13.81	$695.61	$532.85	$139.43 (fourth-graders) $231.55 (seventh-graders)
STUDY SIZE*	1,780 from 22 schools	4,396 from 20 schools	3,495 from 17 schools	8,320 from 63 schools
RESULTS	↑ VERY POSITIVE Paying kids to read dramatically boosted reading-comprehension scores	↔ MIXED Kids cut fewer classes and got slightly better grades. Standardized test scores did not change	↑ POSITIVE Rewarding five different actions, including attendance and behavior, seemed to improve reading skills	↓ NO EFFECT Paying kids for higher test scores did not lead to more learning or better grades—or any other measurable change

*Not including control groups
[†]A combination of metrics that varied from school to school but always included attendance and behavior

Building Word Knowledge

Using Collocations. To write well, select words and expressions that express your meaning accurately and naturally. In English, certain words frequently appear together. These word partners are called "collocations." Here are some examples of collocations from "Is Cash the Answer?"

budget increases: increases in the money allowed to be spent in one year
educational policy: a group of rules and laws that control the educational system
financial incentives: money offered as a way to motivate someone to produce more
full sentences: sentences that have a subject and verb and express a complete idea
good grades: grades that are usually higher than a "C"
standardized tests: tests that are given and scored in a consistent or "standard" way
$20 bill: a piece of U.S. paper money worth twenty dollars

Find the collocations in the reading on page 58. Notice how they are used.

Being Part of the Solution   **59**

Focused Practice

A. *Why did the researchers give students money? Without looking back at the reading, write your answer in a complete sentence.*

Because, the researches don't really know if money works to motivate students to study

B. *Look at the chart on page 59. Then read the statements. Which city does the information refer to? Write D (Dallas), C (Chicago), W (Washington), or N (New York).*

___C___ **1.** Ninth-graders participated in the study.

___C___ **2.** The average student earned more than $600.

___D___ **3.** Paying students dramatically increased reading scores.

___N___ **4.** Paying them to do better on tests didn't have any real effect on test scores.

___C___ **5.** They skipped class less often and got slightly better grades, but their standardized test scores didn't go up.

___C___ **6.** Students got $50 for A's but only $20 for C's.

___N___ **7.** Seventh-graders received $50 to take tests.

___W___ **8.** Students received cash rewards for attendance and good behavior.

___D___ **9.** Students were paid a couple dollars for each book they read.

___W___ **10.** Students could earn as much as $200 a month.

C. *Read the* **Tip for Writers.** *According to the reading, what are the opposing views on the issue of giving cash rewards to students? Complete the sentences with people from the list.*

> **Tip for Writers**
>
> In academic writing, it is important to **be aware of opposing views or opinions**. In a problem-solution essay, you may identify a problem, but someone else might not see it as a problem. Similarly, if you propose a solution, you need to consider possible criticism of your proposal.

| One or more scholars   Children   Parents   Psychologists   Teachers |

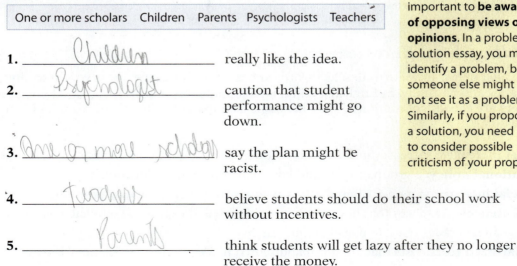

1. ___Children___ really like the idea.

2. ___Psychologist___ caution that student performance might go down.

3. ___One or more scholars___ say the plan might be racist.

4. ___Teachers___ believe students should do their school work without incentives.

5. ___Parents___ think students will get lazy after they no longer receive the money.

D. *Ripley writes, "Over the centuries, the stick (or paddle or switch) has lost favor, in most cases, to the carrot." What is Ripley saying about the way adults motivate children today compared to in the past? Discuss your ideas with a partner.*

E. *Is giving cash incentives to students a good idea? Write one paragraph that gives and explains your opinion.*

I think that giving money for students to study is a bad idea. They should be to motivated in other ways, because the students will grow up thinking that money is everything and they need to learn that life is hard, that will become difficult that the money doesn't solve.

Good
$20.00

Writing a Problem-Solution Essay

In this unit you are going to write a problem-solution essay about a serious problem at school or in the workplace. Problem-solution essays identify and explain a problematic situation and propose a solution. Some problem-solution essays also ask the reader to take action to support a solution.

Like all essays, a problem-solution essay contains three parts.

The Problem-Solution Essay
▶ Introduction
▶ Body
▶ Conclusion

Step 1   Prewriting

For a problem-solution essay, the first prewriting step is to select a topic that you know well enough to describe clearly. Select a problem that you feel is serious and one that can be solved in specific ways. The prewriting step also includes brainstorming about the problem.

You can ask yourself several questions. *Why is it a serious problem? What are its causes and effects? What are some ways to solve the problem? What might critics say about these solutions?* For example, if your topic is low motivation among employees in a company, you might ask yourself: *What effects does low motivation have on the success of the company? Why is motivation so low? What are the most effective ways to increase motivation? What might a critic say about these ways to increase motivation?*

Your Own Writing

Choosing Your Assignment

A. *Choose Assignment 1 or Assignment 2.*

  1. Think of a job environment that you are familiar with. It might be a store, a restaurant, an office, or any workplace you know well. Identify one serious problem in this environment. Propose one or more solutions that might solve the problem.

  2. Think of a school environment that you are familiar with. It could be your current school or a school you attended in the past. Identify one serious problem in this environment. Propose one or more solutions that might solve the problem.

B. *Brainstorm a list of possible problems related to the assignment you chose. Then choose one serious problem from your list and freewrite for ten minutes on your assignment. Here are some questions to get you started:*

  • How did you first become aware of the problem?

  • Why is it a serious problem?

  • What are some causes and effects of the problem?

  • What are some ways to solve the problem? Why do you think the solutions will work?

  • What might critics say about the solutions?

  • What can people do to make the solutions work?

  • What more do you want to find out about the problem before you write your essay?

C. Checking in. *Work with a partner who chose the same assignment. Discuss the ideas and details you wrote in Exercise B. Did your partner . . .*

- describe why it is a serious problem?

- explain the causes and effects of the problem?

- suggest ways to solve or improve the problem?

- write about what critics might say about the solutions?

Share your opinions about your partner's problem and solution. Based on your discussion, make changes and additions to your writing.

D. *Complete the problem-solution chart. List your problem. List some causes and effects of the problem and possible ways to solve or improve it. Fill in as much information as you can. You will have a chance to review, change, or add information later in the unit.*

Brazil

What's the problem?	**Why is this a problem? (effects)**
Violence any cities Education	→ People are dying → → low salary → many kids the same class → teachers with little preparation – family isn't educated

What are some causes of the problem?	**What are some solutions to the problem?**
– lack of control – – family – government – student	– better salaries for teacher and motivate – increase school hours – invest in spots in the school –

THE INTRODUCTION

In Unit 2, you learned that the introductory paragraph of an essay gives important or *background information* to help the reader understand the *thesis statement*.

In a problem-solution essay, the *introduction* gives background information that briefly identifies and describes what the problem is, why it is a serious problem, where it occurs, and whom it affects.

The *thesis statement* will briefly restate the problem. Then the thesis statement will suggest that there are solution(s) that will be discussed in the body of the essay or state specific solution(s) to the problem. As with other essays, the thesis statement may be one or two sentences.

Look at this example of an introductory paragraph from a problem-solution essay:

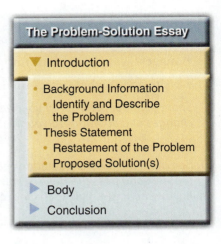

The Problem-Solution Essay

▼ Introduction
  • Background Information
    • Identify and Describe the Problem
  • Thesis Statement
    • Restatement of the Problem
    • Proposed Solution(s)

▶ Body
▶ Conclusion

Example:

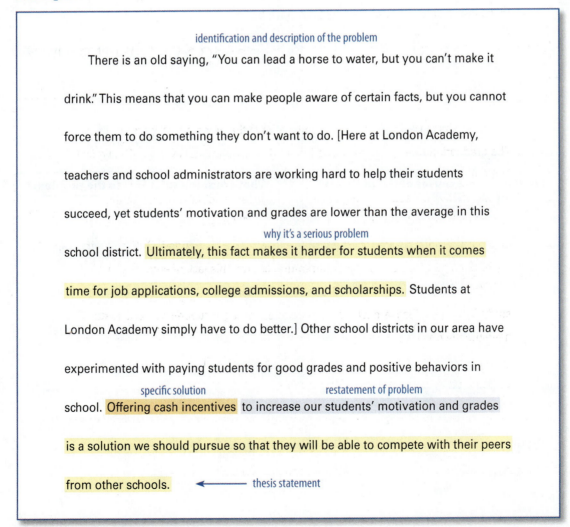

identification and description of the problem

There is an old saying, "You can lead a horse to water, but you can't make it drink." This means that you can make people aware of certain facts, but you cannot force them to do something they don't want to do. [Here at London Academy, teachers and school administrators are working hard to help their students succeed, yet students' motivation and grades are lower than the average in this

why it's a serious problem

school district. Ultimately, this fact makes it harder for students when it comes time for job applications, college admissions, and scholarships. Students at London Academy simply have to do better.] Other school districts in our area have experimented with paying students for good grades and positive behaviors in

specific solution   restatement of problem

school. Offering cash incentives to increase our students' motivation and grades is a solution we should pursue so that they will be able to compete with their peers from other schools. ←——— thesis statement

Focused Practice

Read the following essay assignment and two introductory paragraphs. Then work with a partner. Answer the questions for each paragraph. Give reasons for your answers when you and your partner have different opinions.

Describe a problem at your school and propose one or more solutions.

1.

> No one wants to be a called "low performing," but that's what some people are calling students at Salem Middle School. Recently, the local newspaper reported that Salem's standardized test scores are the lowest of any city in our area. As a result, the school risks losing needed government funding to pay for its academic and sports programs. However this is not just a financial crisis. The test scores indicate that students are not learning what is necessary to be successful in future school years. If their scores are low now, what will happen when they get to high school? Students at Salem Middle School do not have to be low performing now or in the future. There are two ways we can increase student performance and make the future for these students look much brighter.

2.

> Students at Castro Community College have the highest test scores in the city. The graduation rate at Castro is also higher than the national average. The typical student continues on to a four-year college or finds a job upon graduating. These are all positive aspects of being at Castro. However, students report that they cannot wait to graduate because the school is so "lifeless." There is no enthusiasm or group spirit in this school. Sporting events are poorly attended. Only a handful of students participate in clubs or intramural sports. This lack of enthusiasm can also be seen in classrooms. Students seem to just sit there, take notes, and study for exams. Teachers who once tried to encourage students to participate have mostly given up. Now they just lecture. We can greatly increase enthusiasm and improve school spirit if students and teachers are willing to become active participants in the school's daily operation.

1. What is the problem and where is it occuring?
2. Whom is it affecting and why is it a serious problem?
3. Does the thesis statement restate the problem? How?

(continued)

4. Does the thesis statement suggest that there are solutions or propose specific solution(s)?

5. Do you expect to find one or two solutions in the essay? Why?

Your Own Writing

Finding Out More

A. *You may want to learn more about the topic for your essay.*

- If you chose Assignment 1, go to the workplace you are writing about. Interview a variety of people about the problem. As you interview, keep these questions in mind: Why is it a serious problem? Does everyone agree it is a problem? What are the most important causes and effects of the problem? How can the problem best be solved? Take notes.

- If you chose Assignment 2, interview a variety of people at your school about the problem. As you interview, keep these questions in mind: Why is it a serious problem? Does everyone agree it is a problem? What are the most important causes and effects of the problem? How can the problem best be solved? Take notes.

B. *Take notes about what you found out. Record what the people you interviewed said about the problem. Note how their responses were similar and different. Note any new ideas you heard that are relevant to your topic.*

C. **Checking in.** *Share your information with a partner. Did your partner . . .*

- talk to reliable sources of information?

- get important information about the problem and why it is serious?

- get convincing information about solutions to the problem?

Use this information when you write your essay.

Planning Your Introduction

A. *List the background information you will need to include in your introduction.*

_____

_____

_____

_____

B. *Write a draft of your thesis statement. Make sure your thesis statement clearly explains the problem and suggests that there are solutions you will present and justify in the body of your essay. Look back at your freewriting and problem-solution chart to help you.*

_____

_____

C. Checking in. *Share your thesis statement with a partner. Did your partner . . .*

- choose a problem related to school or the workplace?

- clearly restate the problem in the thesis statement?

- suggest that there will be one or more than one solution or propose specific solution(s)?

Tell your partner what you like about his or her thesis statement. If you have any suggestions for improving it, share them. Then tell your partner what kind of supporting evidence you expect to see in his or her essay, based on the thesis statement.

D. *Based on your partner's feedback, you may want to rewrite your thesis statement.*

■ THE BODY

In a problem-solution essay, you begin by convincing your reader that a serious problem exists. You then propose one or more solutions.

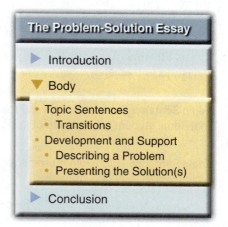

Your essay will follow one of these patterns:

One Solution
Paragraph 1: Introduction + Thesis Statement
Paragraph 2: Discussion of why the problem is serious
Paragraph 3: Solution
Paragraph 4: Conclusion

Multiple Solutions
Paragraph 1: Introduction + Thesis Statement
Paragraph 2: Discussion of why the problem is serious
Paragraph 3: Solution A
Paragraph 4: Solution B
Paragraph 5: Conclusion

Writing Topic Sentences

As you learned in the previous units, each body paragraph must have a topic sentence that presents the controlling idea. In the pattern that you will use for this problem-solution essay, the topic sentence of the first body paragraph will focus on the problem. The topic sentence(s) in the next one or two paragraphs will focus on the solution(s). You will use transitions in your topic sentences to shift the focus from problem to solution or from the first solution to the next.

Presenting the Problem

In the example on page 68, the topic sentence of the first body paragraph includes a transition that moves the focus from the solution proposed in the thesis statement to the problem. To make this transition, the writer restates the problem and then indicates that there are reasons the problem exists.

Thesis Statement: Offering students cash incentives to do better in school is a solution we have to pursue if they are going to be able to compete with their peers from other schools.

transition

Topic Sentence 1: There are several reasons that low performance is a problem, for both the individual student and the school itself.

Proposing One Solution

If you are proposing just *one solution*, the topic sentence in the second body paragraph will include a transition to move the focus from the problem to the solution.

Example:

transition

Topic Sentence 2: To avoid these negative results, the school should use cash incentives to motivate students.

Proposing Multiple Solutions

If your essay contains *two solutions*, your third topic sentence will include a transition to move the focus from the first solution to the second.

Example:

Thesis Statement: In order to motivate students to do better in school, we have to take corrective measures immediately.

transition

Topic Sentence 1: There are several reasons that this lack of motivation is a problem, for both the individual student and the school itself.

transition

Topic Sentence 2: To avoid these negative results, the first thing the school needs to do is try using cash incentives to motivate students.

transition

Topic Sentence 3: In addition to cash incentives, we also need to get parents more involved in the day-to-day activities of the school.

To review transitions, look at Unit 2.

Focused Practice

A. *Read the thesis statements for essays with one solution. For each decide which two topic sentences are best for a four-paragraph essay on this topic. Write 1 next to the first topic sentence (the problem) and 2 next to the second topic sentence (the solution). Then underline the transition part of the sentences you chose. Discuss your answers with a partner.*

Thesis Statement 1: Offering students cash incentives to improve their grades and participation in school activities is a solution we must pursue if London Academy graduates are going to be able to compete with their peers at other schools.

_____ **a.** In a study reported in *Time* magazine, cash incentives were shown to be partially successful in motivating students to do better in school.

_____ **b.** Given the competitive nature of college admissions, we must try a creative solution such as giving students cash rewards to motivate them.

_____ **c.** Colleges look carefully at students' grades and the kinds of extracurricular activities they participate in.

_____ **d.** Whether we like it or not, competition to get into "good" colleges is a serious reality that we cannot ignore.

Thesis Statement 2: School spirit and student participation at Northfield State College are at an all-time low right now, but there are steps we can take to turn this situation around.

_____ **a.** In order to raise spirit and increase participation, students and adults at the school need to be more actively involved in the daily operations of the college.

_____ **b.** This low level of school spirit and participation at Northfield State is a troubling problem for several reasons.

_____ **c.** If students participate in making important decisions at the school, they will feel better about the school itself.

_____ **d.** School administrators, faculty, and parents should encourage students to get involved in sports and after-school clubs.

B. *Read the thesis statements for essays with two solutions. Then decide which three topic sentences are best for a five-paragraph essay on this topic. Write 1 next to the first topic sentence (the problem), 2 next to the second topic sentence (solution A), and 3 next to the third topic sentence (solution B). Then underline the transition part of the sentences you chose. Discuss your answers with a partner.*

Thesis Statement 1: It is not acceptable that students constantly arrive late to class; therefore, the school must take action to fix the problem.

_____ **a.** Second, students need to put pressure on one another to be on time for class.

_____ **b.** When students are late, they distract everyone else in the room, and that is not fair.

_____ **c.** To reduce the number of tardy students, teachers must enforce their late policy and make the consequences of lateness clear and consistent.

_____ **d.** If students are late too often, they also end up missing hours of class time.

(continued)

Thesis Statement 2: Everyone agrees that homework is an important part of learning; however, the excessive amount of homework being assigned here must be limited.

_____ **a.** To be fair to students, teachers need to talk to students about how much time they expect a particular assignment to take.

_____ **b.** No student loves doing homework; however, most will agree that it helps them learn.

_____ **c.** Another way to avoid the negative effects of excessive homework is to give students a detailed syllabus at the beginning of the semester so that they can better plan their time.

_____ **d.** While it would be useless to argue that homework is harmful, there is evidence that too much homework is counterproductive.

Developing a Body Paragraph

As you learned in the previous units, sentences in the body paragraphs support the controlling idea of the paragraph by providing various kinds of supporting details.

In a problem-solution essay, your _first body paragraph_ will explain the _problem_ in greater detail. To do this, consider these questions:

- For whom is it a problem?
- What are some causes of the problem?
- What are some results (effects) of the problem?
- Why is it important to solve the problem?

Your explanation of the problem does not need to answer all of the questions. What is important is that you communicate the message that the problem is serious.

Notice how this thesis statement and example body paragraph present the problem:

Thesis Statement: Offering students cash incentives to improve their grades and participation in school activities is a solution that we must pursue if London Academy graduates are going to be able to compete with their peers from other schools.

> Whether we like it or not, competition to get into "good" colleges is a serious reality that we cannot ignore. It seems to be getting increasingly more difficult for students to get into the colleges they want. First, colleges are looking for accomplished, motivated students who want to be leaders. Students at London Academy do not seem to be developing these qualities. Only four dedicated students actively participate in student government. Colleges also look carefully at students' grades. Last year's records indicate that the majority of students were getting mostly C's in their classes. Furthermore, colleges look not only at students' grades, but also at their extracurricular activities. Records at London Academy
>
> _(continued)_

show that only half of the 500 students in the school participated in one or more extracurricular activities. These facts make it more difficult for students when it comes time to apply to colleges for admission and scholarships. In addition, weak performance and participation by students weakens the overall reputation of the school. When colleges see that students come from a low-ranked high school, they are less likely to admit them. Even the strongest student from a low-ranked school may not be admitted to the best college. Clearly we need to do something.

Notice that in this example, the writer develops this paragraph by explaining why low grades and lack of student participation are a problem. Then the writer supports his explanation with examples and facts. Notice that he also uses the listing order-transition words and phrases *first*, *furthermore*, and *in addition*.

In the *second body paragraph* you will propose a *solution*. Consider these questions to help you present your solution in a clear and convincing way:

- What are the steps or important parts of the solution?
- Why do you think it will work, and what are some specific results you expect to see?

Are there any facts or comments from experts to support your solution?

Given the competitive nature of college admissions, we must try a creative solution such as giving students cash rewards to motivate them. In fact, teens who work hard in school deserve cash incentives. When adults are successful at work, they often get a cash bonus as a reward. This motivates them to work harder. Research shows that a similar approach can help motivate teens to work harder too. According to *Time* magazine, Roland Fryer, Jr. from Harvard University conducted an experiment in which he gave cash incentives to students in four cities. In Dallas, cash incentives helped second-graders to become better readers. In Chicago, ninth-graders went to class more often and got better grades. In Washington, D.C. students' attendance, behavior, and reading skills all improved. The results were not always positive, but they were never negative. At London Academy we can start by offering a bonus to students who improve their grade by one full grade each semester. We can give an additional bonus to the student with the highest average in his or her class. Students who take an active role or leadership position in certain extracurricular activities can also receive a cash incentive. With the right incentive, increased student motivation and improved performance can become achievable goals.

Notice how the writer describes the solution in this example of a body paragraph. In the topic sentence, the writer presents the solution to the problem. The writer then develops and supports his idea with reasons he thinks the solution will work, steps needed to implement the solution, and anticipated results.

If your essay contains more than one solution, each remaining body paragraph will propose an additional solution and provide examples, facts, and other relevant information to support your proposal. Each topic sentence in these paragraphs should contain a transition that helps move the focus of the essay from one solution to the next.

Focused Practice

Read the thesis statement and two body paragraphs. Then answer the questions and discuss your answers with a partner.

Thesis Statement: School spirit and student participation at Northfield State College are at an all-time low right now, but there are steps we can take to turn this situation around.

Body Paragraph 1

The low level of school spirit and participation at Northfield State is a troubling problem for several reasons. If you think about it, increasing student involvement is in some ways just as important as the academics. By not participating in the life of the school, students are missing out on valuable life lessons—lessons that they need to be productive members of their community or workplace after college. Students need to understand that communities function only through the active efforts of its members. By getting involved, students also learn important leadership skills that will help them advance in their careers, whether they choose to work in a grocery store, a school, or a large company. Few Northfield students seem to be demonstrating these skills. Last semester only a handful of students ran for seats on the student government. Clubs and extracurricular activities are disappearing because of lack of participation. As a result, so is the funding. School sporting events are demoralizing for players because there are no fans there to cheer for them. It is not surprising that few of our teams have winning records. Furthermore, this situation is a problem not only for the student body, but also for the college. Prospective students will be less interested in attending Northfield State if it has a reputation for low levels of school spirit and participation. Thus, students today have an impact on how people will view the school in the future. Students choose a college not only for the academics, but also for the larger college experience. If we want to offer our students the "full" college experience, then something needs to be done.

1. What is the problem?

2. For whom is it a problem?

3. What are some results (effects) of the problem?

4. Why is it important to solve the problem?

Body Paragraph 2

> In order to raise spirit and participation, students need to be more actively involved in the daily operation of the college. First of all, events like orientation meetings for new students and graduation should be organized in collaboration with the school's administration and faculty. Students need to take an active role in planning and publicizing these events. This active involvement would definitely lead to increased participation. Second, school events, such as sporting events and theater productions should be widely publicized throughout the school and local community, and on the school website. Student attendance at all of these events must be enthusiastically encouraged, and to further build school spirit, faculty and staff should also attend. In addition, the student government should be given a voice in important school decisions that affect them directly. For example, they might get involved in choosing courses to update the curriculum or sit on committees to hire new faculty members. Finally, and perhaps most important, all members of the school community must engage in an honest conversation about why school spirit is so low. The faculty and administration may be unaware of the specific reasons for this lack of enthusiasm. Once key issues are identified, the entire school community will be able to work together to solve the problem more easily. When students realize that the key to an enjoyable college experience is to be actively involved, rather than simply to show up, they will see that participation is critical for developing school spirit and that greater spirit promotes enthusiastic participation. As the saying goes, "If you're not part of the solution, you're part of the problem."

1. What are the steps or important parts of the solution?

2. Why does the writer think the solution will work?

3. What are some specific results the writer expects to see?

4. What transition words or phrases does the writer use? Underline them.

Your Own Writing

Planning Your Body Paragraphs

A. *Before you begin writing your body paragraphs, complete the outline below. Copy your thesis statement from page 66.*

- Write a topic sentence for each of the body paragraphs.
- Provide details that develop and support the controlling idea of each topic sentence.

Problem-Solution Essay

▶ Thesis Statement: _____

_____

▶ Body Paragraph 1

   ▶ Topic Sentence: _____

   _____

      ▶ Supporting Details:

         • _____

         • _____

▶ Body Paragraph 2

   ▶ Topic Sentence: _____

   _____

      ▶ Supporting Details:

         • _____

         • _____

▶ Body Paragraph 3 (for an essay with more than one solution)

   ▶ Topic Sentence: _____

   _____

      ▶ Supporting Details:

         • _____

         • _____

■ THE CONCLUSION

As in other academic essays, in the conclusion to a problem-solution essay, you return to your thesis statement. You will clearly restate the problem and proposed solution(s) and then end your essay with a concluding strategy. Here are two concluding strategies that you may want to use to end your essay.

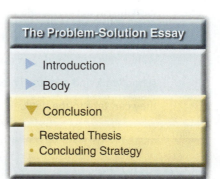

1. Counterargument

2. Call to action

As you learned in Unit 2, strong writers acknowledge opposing views or perspectives in their essays. However, when you present the views of your critics—those who disagree with your proposed solution—you also need to defend your view. A *counterargument* is your defense.

To present a counterargument, briefly present your opponent's view. Then explain why yours is still the best solution. If you agree with part of your opponent's view, then you can say so. This is called a *concession*. However, you ultimately explain why your solution is better or stronger.

In the following example, notice how the writer acknowledges the opposing view, offers a concession, and then explains why his proposed solution is best.

In an ideal world, we would not be discussing paying students to motivate them. Critics of this solution argue that paying students to do what they should do of their own volition is a serious problem. They believe that studying is a student's job, and that moving up to the next grade and eventually graduating is his or her ultimate reward. It sounds good in theory, but in practice it is not working. Students at London Academy do not think about graduation as much as they think about life after graduation. Perhaps graduating does not feel like a reward to them. Students at this school are not doing as well as they need to be doing. As educators, we ought to be much more creative about solutions to this problem. Paying students to work harder is a creative solution that can work. Students will do their schoolwork and eventually learn that hard work pays off in a practical way that they can take to the bank.

In a *call to action* tell your audience how they can actively get involved. When you do this, focus on specific groups of people and tell them specifically how they should take action in order to make your solution happen. Notice how the writer does this in the following example.

> In an ideal world, we would not be discussing paying students to motivate them. However, this is the real world, and it is a world in which money talks. The fact is that students at this school are not doing as well as they need to be doing. If we want the best future for our children we should not delay in implementing a plan for cash incentives. Paying students to work harder is a creative solution that can work. Parents need to contact their schools and encourage them to get working on it. School administrators and faculty need to put a reward system in place. With students' input, they should decide on what changes or behaviors will be rewarded and how much each change will be worth. Students will do their schoolwork and eventually learn that hard work pays off in a practical way that they can take to the bank.

Focused Practice

A. *Work with a partner. Read the three proposed solutions. Then, write what critics might say about the solutions and give a counterargument to show that the proposed solution is a good one. The first one is done for you.*

Proposed Solution	What the Critics Say	Your Counterargument
To help students keep up with homework assignments, professors should only give one hour of homework for every hour that the class meets.	This idea will never work because some assignments, such as an essay, naturally take more time to do.	One assignment can be given over several days. Professors can choose their assignments carefully and not assign time-consuming tasks that are less important.
To increase school spirit and involvement, the school should pay students to attend school events, such as sports and theater productions.		
To reduce tardiness, professors should deduct five points from a student's final course grade each time he or she is late to class.		

B. *Complete the chart with a solution for each problem. Explain who needs to get involved and what they should do. Then work with a partner and compare your charts.*

Problem	Solution	Who should get involved?	What should they do?
Student test scores are too low.	Pay students as an incentive to study harder.	Parents, teachers, and students	All: Decide on changes they want and what incentives might help them achieve this goal
Students are not completing their homework.		Parents, teachers and students	Parents: Students: Teachers:
Lateness in the morning has become a serious a problem.			

C. *Read the following essay assignment and the concluding paragraph. Then discuss the questions with a partner.*

Describe a problem in your college and propose one or more solutions.

> In conclusion, if we are going to solve the problem of students not completing their homework assignments, there must be a clear, consistent policy regarding late or missing assignments. The most important part of this policy should be that if students are late handing in two homework assignments, their final grade in the course will drop by ten percent and by five percent for every late or missing assignment after that. The faculty must take the lead in this effort. Beginning next semester, they must inform students of this policy and then enforce it consistently. Once all faculty members follow the same procedures regarding homework, students will get the message and complete their assignments on time. If we are going to make positive changes, we all need to be on the same page.

1. What was the problem discussed in this essay? Write it here: _____

2. What was the solution? Write it here: _____

3. What is the writer's restated thesis? Circle the sentence.

4. Which concluding strategy did the writer use? _____

D. *Rewrite the concluding paragraph in Exercise C on page 77. Use a concluding strategy different from the one that the writer used. Then share your paragraph with a partner.*

> In conclusion, if we are going to solve the problem of students not completing their homework assignments, there must be a clear, consistent policy regarding late or missing assignments. The most important part of this policy will be that if students are late handing in two homework assignments, their final grade in the course will drop by ten percent and by five percent for every late or missing assignment after that.
>
> _____
>
> _____
>
> _____
>
> _____
>
> _____

Your Own Writing

Planning Your Conclusion

A. *How will you rephrase your thesis statement in the conclusion? List your ideas here.*

_____

_____

B. *What strategy will you use to close the essay?*

_____

_____

C. Checking in. *Share your ideas with a partner. Did your partner . . .*

- discover a new and interesting way to phrase the thesis statement?

- choose an effective concluding strategy?

Writing Your First Draft

Read the Tip for Writers. *Review your notes on pages 63, 66, and 74. Then write the first draft of your essay. When you are finished, give your essay a working title. Hand in your draft to your teacher.*

Tip for Writers

As you write your first draft, be sure that you have **considered opposing views**.

Revising your work is an essential part of the writing process. This is your opportunity to be sure that your essay has all of the important pieces and that it is clear.

Focused Practice

A. *You have read parts of this problem-solution essay already. Now read the entire essay to see how the parts fit together.*

Going for the Long-Term Payoff

There is an old saying, "You can lead a horse to water, but you can't make it drink." This means that you can make people aware of certain facts, but you cannot force them to do something they don't want to do. Here at London Academy, teachers and school administrators are working hard to help their students succeed, yet students' motivation and grades are lower than the average in this school district. Ultimately, this fact makes it harder for students when it comes time for job applications, college admissions, and scholarships. Students at London Academy simply have to do better. Other school districts in our area have experimented with paying students for good grades and positive behaviors in school. Offering cash incentives to increase our students' motivation and grades is a solution we should pursue so that they will be able to compete with their peers from other schools.

Whether we like it or not, competition to get into "good" colleges is a serious reality that we cannot ignore. It seems to be getting increasingly more difficult for students to get into the colleges they want. First, colleges are looking for accomplished, motivated students who want to be leaders. Students at London Academy do not seem to be developing these qualities. Only four dedicated students actively participate in student government. Colleges also look carefully at students' grades. Last year's records indicate that the majority of students were getting mostly C's in their classes. Furthermore, colleges look not only at students' grades, but also at their extracurricular activities. Records at London Academy show that only half of the 500 students in the school participated in one or more extracurricular activity. These facts make it more difficult for students when it comes time to apply to colleges for admission and scholarships. In addition, weak performance and participation by students weakens the overall reputation of the school. When colleges see that students come from a low-ranked high school, they

(continued)

---

are less likely to admit them. Even the strongest student from a low-ranked school may not be admitted to the best colleges. Clearly we need to do something.

Given the competitive nature of college admissions, we must try a creative solution such as giving students cash rewards to motivate them. In fact, teens who work hard in school deserve cash incentives. When adults are successful at work, they often get a cash bonus as a reward. This motivates them to work harder. Research shows that a similar approach can help motivate teens to work harder too. According to *Time* magazine, Roland Fryer, Jr. from Harvard University conducted an experiment in which he gave cash incentives to students in four cities. In Dallas, cash incentives helped second-graders to become better readers. In Chicago, ninth-graders went to class more often and got better grades. In Washington, D.C. students' attendance, behavior, and reading skills all improved. The results were not always positive, but they were never negative. At London Academy we can start by offering a bonus to students who raise their averages by one full grade each semester, for example from a C to a B. We can give an additional bonus to the student with the highest average in his or her class. Students who take an active role or leadership positions in certain extracurricular activities can also receive a cash incentive. With the right incentive, increased student motivation and improved performance can become achievable goals.

In an ideal world, we would not be discussing paying students to motivate them. Critics of this solution argue that paying students to do what they should do of their own volition is a serious problem. They believe that studying is a student's job, and that passing to the next grade and eventually graduating is his or her ultimate reward. This sounds good in theory, but in practice it is not working. Students at London Academy do not think about graduation as much as they think about life after graduation. Perhaps graduating does not feel like a reward to them. Students at this school are not doing as well as they need to be doing. As educators, we ought to be much more creative about solutions to this problem. Paying students to work harder is a creative solution that can work. Parents need to contact their schools and encourage them to get working on it. School administrators and faculty need to put a reward system in place. With the input of students, they should decide on what changes or behaviors will be rewarded and how much each of these changes will be worth. Students will do their schoolwork and eventually learn that hard work pays off in a practical way that they can take to the bank.

B. *Work with a partner. Answer these questions about the essay.*

1. What kinds of background information appear in the introduction? Check (✓) sentences that provide background information.

2. Underline the thesis statement. What is the problem it states? What is the proposed solution?

   _____

   _____

3. Does the first body paragraph explain the solution in detail? What kinds of supporting details does the writer provide? Label them as *examples, facts,* or *comments from experts.*

4. Double underline the topic sentences for the body paragraphs and the restated thesis in the conclusion. How are these sentences related?

   _____

   _____

5. In the body paragraph that describes a solution for the problem, what specific step(s)

   does the writer suggest should be taken to implement the solution? _____

   _____

   _____

   _____

   _____

6. What concluding strategy does the writer use to finish the essay? Is it effective? Why?

   _____

   _____

   _____

C. Checking in. *Discuss your marked-up essay with another pair of students. Then in your group, share one thing about the essay that you found the most interesting. Explain your answer.*

Building Word Knowledge

Using Collocations. The writer included some collocations in "Going for the Long-Term Payoff," including *school district, job applications, college admissions, cash incentive, achievable goals,* and *reading skills.*

Complete each sentence with a collocation from the list.

cash refund	college tuition	four-year college	job search	long-term goal
cash reward	community college	goal-oriented	job security	short-term goal

1. My roommate left a laptop computer on the bus. He was offering a

   _____ to anyone who returned it.

2. Nan knows what she wants and how to get it. She is very _____.

3. In the United States, some students start at a two-year

   _____ and then transfer to a _____.

4. There isn't a lot of _____ in my company. Employees never

   know when they might be laid off and have to look for something else.

5. My _____ is to become a biochemist. Before I do that, I

   have to get into a good college and study science.

6. Eventually I want to run my own business, but for now my _____ is to

get work experience and save some money.

7. If you buy a jacket and then decide that you don't like it, you can return it the next day for a

_____ or a store credit.

8. It's very difficult for families to save enough money to pay their children's

_____. Scholarships and student loans may help.

9. My _____ is going really well. I have three interviews next week.

Your Own Writing

Revising Your Draft

A. *Reread the first draft of your essay. Use the Revision Checklist to identify parts of your writing that might need improvement.*

B. *Review your plans and notes and your responses to the Revision Checklist. Then revise your first draft. Save your revised essay. You will look at it again in the next section.*

Revision Checklist

Did you . . .

☐ identify and explain the problem in the introduction?

☐ include a thesis statement that restates the problem and proposes a solution?

☐ clearly show why the problem is serious in the first body paragraph?

☐ propose and explain at least one solution?

☐ offer supporting examples, facts, or comments from experts?

☐ return to the main idea in your thesis statement to signal the end of your essay?

☐ use a concluding strategy to end your essay?

☐ use collocations correctly?

☐ give your essay an interesting title?

Step 4 Editing

■ GRAMMAR PRESENTATION

Before you hand in your revised essay, you must check it for any errors in grammar, punctuation, and spelling. In this section you will learn about modals. You will focus on this grammar when you edit and proofread your essay.

Modals

Grammar Notes	Examples
1. Modals are auxiliary ("helping") verbs. Use modals to express	
a. social functions such as describing **ability**, giving **advice**, and expressing **necessity**	• We **can learn** from others' experience. • They **should consider** other solutions.
b. logical possibilities such as drawing **conclusions** and talking about **future possibilities**	• A student **must participate** in other activities. • She **might have** a better solution.
REMEMBER: Modals have **only one form**. They do not have *–s* in the third person singular. Always use **modal + base form** of the verb.	Not: She ~~mights~~ have a better solution. Not: She ~~might to~~ have a better solution.
2. Use the following **modals** for **ability**:	
a. *can* or *be able to* for **present ability** **USAGE NOTE:** *Can* is more common than *be able to* in the present.	• "You **can lead** a horse to water but you **can't make** it drink."
b. *could* or *was/were able to* for **past ability**	• Young **could** (not) **pass** the reading test. • Rosa **was** (not) **able to pass** her reading test.
c. *can* or *will be/be going to be able to* for **future ability** **REMEMBER:** Use the correct form of *be able to* for all other verb forms.	• With her record, Sharon **can get** into a good college. • With her record, Sharon **will be able to get** into a good college. • With her record, Sharon **is going to be able to get** into a good college.

3. Use the following **modals** for **advice**:

a. *should* and *ought to* to give advice

Usage Note: *Should* is much more common that *ought to*. Also, *ought to* is not used in the negative.

- We **should** (not) **study** harder next semester.
- We **ought to study** harder next semester.

b. *had better* for **urgent advice**—when you believe that something bad will happen if the person does not follow the advice.

- We **had better study** harder or else we'll lose our scholarships.

c. *shouldn't* and *had better not* for **negative advice**.

- You **shouldn't miss** class again. You need to pass this exam!
- You **had better not miss** class again!

4. Use the following **modals** for **necessity**:

a. *have to* and *have got to* (in conversation and in informal writing)

- Siu **has to study** for the midterm exam this weekend. She doesn't feel ready.

Usage Note: We often use *have got to* to express strong feelings.

- I **have got to study** for the midterm exam this weekend. I don't feel ready!

b. *must* (in writing such as official forms, signs, and manuals)

- We **must** take action now.

5. Use the following **modals** for **future possibility:** *may (not)*, *might (not)*, and *could* to express the possibility that something **will** or **will not happen**. The three modals have very similar meanings.

- Your classmates **may** (not) **enjoy** your presentation.
- Your classmates **might** (not) **enjoy** your presentation.
- Your classmates **could enjoy** your presentation.

Be Careful! Do not use *couldn't* for future possibility. *Couldn't* means that something is **impossible**.

- Eugene **couldn't go** shopping on Sunday night. The shops were closed.

Focused Practice

A. *Look back at the essay on page 79.*

- Scan the text for examples of the modal verbs presented in the chart.
- Circle the modal verbs together with the base form of the verb.
- Decide whether each modal expresses ability, advice, necessity, or future possibility.

Then discuss your answers with a partner.

B. *Complete each sentence with a modal and the verb provided. Express the idea in parentheses at the end of each sentence.*

1. This store's profits _____ dramatically if they offered
   (increase)
   special deals daily. (future possibility)

2. The management _____ something about office morale.
   (do)
   The employees are not happy with the way things are. (urgent advice)

3. Second-graders _____ ten books in one week. (ability)
   (not / read)

4. Schools _____ students for doing schoolwork well. (advice)
   (pay)

5. We _____ the deadline for the scholarship application.
   (not / miss)
   (urgent advice)

6. If they are not careful, the "worst-case scenario" _____
   (happen)
   (future possibility)

7. The school _____ students have textbooks for free. (advice)
   (let)

8. We simply _____ this situation get out of hand. (ability)
   (not / allow)

9. Seventh-graders _____ well behaved. We
   (be)
   _____ them for good behavior. (advice)
   (not / pay)

10. The team _____ easily _____ this
    (overcome)
    problem if everyone works together. (ability)

C. *Read and edit the paragraph. There are seven errors in the use of modals. The first error has been corrected for you. Find and correct six more.*

> If schools give students cash incentives, everyone wins. Students win because
> they will have external motivation to do better even if they don't have a strong
> internal motivation. They may discovering that they are better students than
> they thought. This might leads to the students' becoming self-motivated. Parents
> win because they will no longer worry if their children are doing their best. Back
> when their kids were very little, they can tell them what to do and the kids would
> listen. Once they go to school, this becomes more difficult. With this business-like
> agreement, parents have to complain less and simply be proud of their children's
> success. Schools will win, too. Increased student performance will raise the
> ranking of the school. They could receive positive publicity, and they might even
>
> *(continued)*

get money from the city or state to pay for school programs. In fact, the mayor of this city recently announced that the city currently has the money to pay for these incentives. We had better to take the opportunity before it is too late. We could not miss this opportunity, or we ought to regret it in the future.

D. Write five sentences related to the topic you chose on page 62. Use modals. These may be sentences you already have in your essay. Then indicate whether each sentence shows ability (AB), advice (AD), necessity (NE), or future possibility (FP).

_____ 1. _____

_____

_____ 2. _____

_____

_____ 3. _____

_____

_____ 4. _____

_____

_____ 5. _____

_____

Your Own Writing

Editing Your Draft

A. Use the Editing Checklist to edit and proofread your essay.

B. Prepare a clean copy of the final draft of your essay and hand it in to your teacher.

Editing Checklist
Did you . . .
☐ use a variety of modals?
☐ use correct verb forms, punctuation, and spelling?
☐ use collocations and other words correctly?
☐ consider opposing views?

IN THIS UNIT You will be writing an essay about the similarities or differences between one time in life and another.

The U.S. statesman, scientist, and philosopher Benjamin Franklin (1706–1793) once said, "When you're finished changing, you're finished." Franklin is reminding us that change in life is both necessary and inevitable—you can't avoid it. However, even though change is part of life, it is not always easy to face. What important changes have you seen in your lifetime?

Planning for Writing

■ BRAINSTORM

A. *Inventions can change people's lives in significant ways. What did people do before the arrival of the inventions in the chart? Discuss your answers with a partner.*

Invention	What did people do before?
1. credit cards	Pay with check or money
2. cars	by horses
3. computers	use more paper
4. the Internet	check information in books
5. cell phones	use more letters and mails

B. Using a Compare-Contrast Chart. When you write about what life was like before or after a big change, you can use a T-chart to record similarities and/or differences between one or more things in the two time periods.

Work with a partner. Think about the effects of these inventions. What are the positive effects? What are the negative effects?

Invention	Positive Effects	Negative Effects
1. credit cards	*Doing business is much more convenient.*	*People spend more than they can afford.*
2. cars	- Fast - Convenient	- Expensive - Insurance
3. computers	Games	Addict
4. the Internet	Fast news	Fakes new
5. cell phones	Conect	Addict

Read the blog about life before and after the arrival of the Internet.

TALK OF THE TIMES A Weekly Blog about Daily Life

By Chelsea Pierce

The Good Old Days

1 My grandfather was somewhat of a curmudgeon[1]— always complaining, especially about the way things have changed. To him, things were much better in the "good old days."

2 For Grandpa, TV was simply a force of evil in the house. Nothing good could come of it. Back in *his* day, he claimed, children found their own ways to amuse themselves. If they wanted a story, they read books or made up stories of their own. They spent most of their time running around outside with friends and maybe even getting into trouble every once in a while.

3 Even though I don't want to be a curmudgeon like Grandpa, sometimes I feel myself heading in that direction, especially when it comes to the Internet and mobile technology, like smartphones[2] for instance.

4 Don't get me wrong, I use the Internet and my smartphone, and I appreciate them very much, but sometimes I also like to look back at what my life was like before these technologies came along. It seems like it was a simpler time.

5 Back then I used to read books much more often—I guess my grandfather would be proud to hear me say that. I used to love to go to the library or a bookstore, look through the long rows of fiction and nonfiction, and find a book I could get lost in for a while. Today I rarely get to the library, and a lot of the bookstores in my neighborhood have closed. If I want a book, I usually order it online and wait for it to arrive, or I download an e-book onto my e-reader.[3] That's pretty convenient. Still, I prefer the feel and smell of the pages of a book. Reading a book is more satisfying than reading from a computer screen. I miss being able to slip a paperback into my pocket and pull it out while waiting for a bus or eating lunch. Pulling out my laptop or e-reader doesn't give me the same pleasure. Besides, at the end of a long day at work, when I want to read and relax, the last thing that I want to do is stare at a computer screen.

6 Speaking of work, I can safely say that with my computer I can go almost an entire day without speaking to any of the hundred plus people in my office. People who sit two cubicles away use email instead of calling or good old-fashioned getting up and walking over to talk. I've fallen into the same habit too because it seems more efficient. Then I wonder, has the Internet really brought people closer together, or has it kept us farther apart?

7 That's the interesting thing about the Internet. Sometimes it feels like a series of contrasts. Even though communication with my co-workers might have lost that "personal" touch, today I often feel even more connected to the world around me. The Internet has made sharing ideas much easier, and my ways of thinking and my awareness of the world have broadened.[4] I can now sit at my desk and interact with people from all over the world, finding out what they're thinking and what their lives are like.

---

[1] **curmudgeon:** an old person who is often angry and annoyed
[2] **smartphone:** a cellular or mobile phone that has Internet capabilities
[3] **e-reader:** a portable electronic device that is used to read digital books and periodicals
[4] **broadened:** become larger and wider

8 Even as I write this, I think about my grandfather. He didn't live long enough to see the Internet, but I can just imagine what he's thinking about it, and it's not good—not like the good old days, that's for sure!

9 Soon people won't even remember what life was like before the Internet, but we're living in very special times, watching a revolution unfold right before our very eyes. I know I'm not alone in the new digital world, so let me turn the discussion over to the rest of you out there in cyberspace.[5]

10 How has the Internet influenced your life or changed the way *you* think?

COMMENTS:

11 As my grandmother used to say, "The only good thing about the good old days is that they're gone."
LBG
Austin, Texas, USA Posted 11/20 at 6:00 AM

12 It's a struggle. Unlike my teenage kids, who don't think twice about using new technology, I have a love-hate relationship with it. The Internet offers many conveniences—I order my groceries online these days—but I also waste a lot of time staring at the images on the screen.
ModernMom
Melbourne, Australia Posted 11/22 at 7:30 PM

13 Chelsea, I agree with what you said about communication. The Internet has really changed the way I communicate with people. I work from home and live alone. The Internet has brought me friendships and business opportunities that I wouldn't have found otherwise.
Mario
Mexico City Posted 11/24 at 9:00 AM

14 Chelsea, you've inspired me to turn off my computer and go outside and play with my dog, Rex. I have to use the Internet to run my home business. As someone who spends hours in front of the computer, I sometimes feel as if I'm living in a virtual[6] world. Your blog reminds me that real life is still out there! Thanks for the post!
Koji Yamamoto
New York, NY Posted 11/24 at 9:30 AM

15 I've never really thought about how the Internet has changed my life because I'm so used to the technology now. I guess it *is* easier to communicate on the Web, but it's not necessarily better.
Sassy@miamimail.com
Miami Beach, FL Posted 11/25 at 8:10 PM

16 What are you talking about??? How *old* are you people anyway??? The Internet is part of our daily life. Period. Most of your readers probably can't remember a time without it! It's time to stop talking about life without it and just accept it. Move on!
Colinski@uaeb.net Posted 11/26 at 3:00 AM

17 As a full-time student, I couldn't imagine going back to the days before the Internet. Today I take many classes online. I communicate with professors through quick emails. I can take tests and quizzes online so we don't waste class time. Life for us students would be much more difficult without the Internet.
Natayada
Bangkok, Thailand Posted 11/26 at 6:20 PM

Post a new comment:
_____

[5] **cyberspace:** all the connections between computers in different places, considered as a real place where information, messages, pictures, etc., exist
[6] **virtual:** something that is done on a computer rather than in the real world

Building Word Knowledge

Using New Words. Just as technology is always changing, so is language. New words are formed and existing words are used in new ways. To write well, you must learn the "new" words that have entered the language in recent years. Computer technology alone has introduced many new words into English. It is important to know what these words mean so that you can use them correctly in your writing. Words, such as *texting, cyberspace,* and *the Web,* are very common and are in most large dictionaries.

Find the following "new" words in the reading on page 90. Notice how they are used. Then write a sentence for each word.

1. blog _We can get many ideas from blogs_

2. mobile technology _I con talk with my friends everywhere_

3. e-reader _____

4. laptop _I can do my homework fast with my laptop_

5. virtual _____

6. cyberspace _We con be connect everywhere connect between computers_

Focused Practice

A. *Answer each question in a complete sentence. Discuss your answers with a partner.*

1. According to Chelsea's grandfather, how did children entertain themselves in the past?

   They play together

   _____

2. Why does Chelsea spend less time in bookstores today?

   _____

   _____

3. Which does Chelsea prefer, books or e-books? Why?

   _____

   _____

4. How does Chelsea communicate with her co-workers today?

   _____

   _____

5. According to Chelsea, what positive changes has the Internet brought to her life?

_____

_____

6. Why is Chelsea thinking about her grandfather as she is writing?

_____

_____

B. *Read the comments. Which comment would the person probably make? Write the letter on the line.*

_____ **1.** Chelsea Pierce
　　　a. I plan to give up my smartphone.
　　　b. I feel the same way my grandfather did about change.
　　　c. I have mixed feelings about the Internet.

_____ **2.** LBG
　　　a. Don't look back at the past. Just keep up with the times.
　　　b. The good old days were better than today.
　　　c. Your past determines what kind of person you are today.

_____ **3.** ModernMom
　　　a. I think the Internet has both advantages and disadvantages.
　　　b. I'm just like my children when it comes to using the Internet.
　　　c. I don't think twice about using new technology.

_____ **4.** Mario
　　　a. I had a better personal and professional life when I worked in an office.
　　　b. I feel more isolated because of the way people communicate online now.
　　　c. I'm thankful for the opportunities the Internet offers me personally and professionally.

_____ **5.** Koji Yamamoto
　　　a. I'll probably read this blog in the future.
　　　b. I'll probably get another dog.
　　　c. I'll probably try to find a new job in the near future.

_____ **6.** Sassy
　　　a. I'm not completely satisfied with communication online.
　　　b. It's much more difficult to communicate online than in person.
　　　c. I often think about the impact the Internet has had on my life.

_____ **7.** Colinski
　　　a. I am too old to learn how to use technology.
　　　b. I'm annoyed that the Internet is such an influential part of daily life.
　　　c. I'm annoyed by people who resist technological advancements.

_____ **8.** Natayada
　　　a. I would like to go back to the days before the Internet.
　　　b. The Internet is an integral part of our lives now.
　　　c. The Internet has taken over my life.

C. Read the **Tip for Writers.** *Then read each set of statements. Is the language formal or informal? Write* I *(informal) or* F *(formal). Discuss your answers with a partner.*

_____ **1.** Prior to the advent of the Internet, people were much more likely to read books. They frequently visited libraries and bookstores, where they would peruse the long rows of fiction and nonfiction in order to find the perfect book.

_____ **2.** Back then I used to read books a lot more—I guess my grandfather would be proud to hear me say that. I used to love going to the library or to a bookstore, looking through the long rows of fiction and nonfiction, and finding a book I could get lost in for a while.

_____ **3.** Unlike my teenage kids, who don't think twice about using new technology, I have a love-hate relationship with it. The Internet is convenient—that's for sure. I even order my groceries online these days. I also waste a lot of time staring at the images on the screen.

_____ **4.** Unlike teenagers, who cannot imagine life without modern technology, many older adults have a more conflicted relationship with the Internet. While they embrace the speed and convenience, they often long for the days when things, to them at least, were simpler.

_____ **5.** There are a number of advantages and disadvantages associated with the Internet. People are now able to do essential banking online and shop without the inconvenience leaving home. However, there are also the risks of becoming addicted and visiting websites that make them vulnerable in a variety of ways.

_____ **6.** Chelsea, you're right on with what you said about communication. The Internet really changed the way that I communicate with people. I work from home and live alone. Through the Internet, I have made friends and made business connections I wouldn't have otherwise.

D. *How has the Internet influenced your life or changed the way you think? Write your own response to the blog post. Before you begin, think about your writing style: will it be formal or informal? Try to use "new words" in your writing.*

_____

_____

_____

_____

_____

> ### Tip for Writers
>
> When you write, **think about your language style**, or level of formality. Informal writing usually contains more casual language—words and expressions used in everyday speech. It may include slang expressions, idioms, contractions, and/or abbreviations. Formal writing frequently contains longer academic words, such as *consume* (instead of *eat*) or *detect* (instead of *find*) and more complex sentence structure. For emails, blogs, and personal letters, an informal style is often fine. For academic writing your style will usually be more formal and serious.

Writing a Compare-Contrast Essay

You are going to write an essay that compares or contrasts your experiences before and after a significant change in your life. When you compare, you show how two people, things, or ideas are similar. When you contrast, you show how they are different. In this compare-contrast essay about two different time periods, you will describe the specific ways the two periods were alike or different.

> ### The Compare-Contrast Essay
> ▶ Introduction
> ▶ Body
> ▶ Conclusion

Like all essays, a compare-contrast essay contains three parts.

Step 1   Prewriting

For a compare-contrast essay, the prewriting step involves selecting two people, things, or ideas that have clear similarities and/or differences. It also includes thinking about specific points of comparison and contrast. In this unit, the term "points of comparison" will also mean points of contrast.

Cell Phones

Your Own Writing

Choosing Your Assignment

A. *Choose Assignment 1 or Assignment 2.*

1. Compare or contrast life before and after an important invention. Choose an invention that happened in your lifetime, but don't choose a broad topic, such as the Internet. For example, you might write about life before and after the invention of laptops, cell phones, MP3 players, or Facebook.™

2. Compare or contrast life before and after a significant event. For example, you could write about life before and after people get married, graduate from high school or college, or move to a new place.

B. *Freewrite for ten minutes on your assignment. Here are some questions to get you started:*

- Why is this invention or event important?

- What was life like before this invention or event?

- What was it like after?

- Were the changes positive or negative or a combination of both?

C. **Checking in.** *Work with a partner who chose the same assignment. Discuss the ideas and details you wrote in Exercise B. Did your partner . . .*

- choose a life-changing invention or event that has clear similarities or differences?

- describe what life was like before and after the invention or event occurred?

- explain whether the changes have been positive or negative?

Based on your discussion, make changes and additions to your writing.

D. *Complete the T-chart. List details about your life before and after the invention or event. Fill in as much information as you can. You will have a chance to review, change, or add information later in the unit.*

Invention or Event: _____	
Before	**After**
1.	1.
2.	2.
3.	3.
4.	4.

■ THE INTRODUCTION

As you learned in Units 2 and 3, the introductory paragraph of an essay contains two parts: *background information* and a *thesis statement*.

In Unit 2 you learned that the background information helps the reader understand the thesis statement.

In a compare-contrast essay, the thesis statement usually presents what will be compared and/or contrasted in the body of the essay. The thesis statement also identifies the specific points of comparison that the essay will cover. The thesis statement may also include an opinion, for example, whether something is positive, negative, or a combination of both. As in most essays, the thesis statement may be one or two sentences.

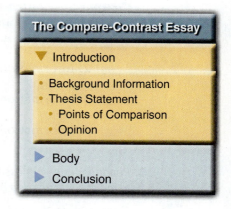

When you read the following thesis statements for an introductory paragraph, you can see the differences between a strong thesis and a weak one. The first two examples clearly indicate that something before and after an invention or event is being compared. These examples also give clear points of comparison and offer an opinion. The last two statements identify the topic, but state no points of comparison or opinion.

Examples:

Strong: After I bought my first computer, my way of doing things changed completely and for the better. I now use the computer to keep in touch with people, store important documents and photos, and handle my finances.

(**What is being compared:** ways of doing things before/after buying a computer; **three clear points of comparison:** keeping in touch, storing information, handling finances; **opinion:** the change was good)

Strong: When I compare life before and after having kids, I think that children give one an important purpose in life, which includes new responsibilities, interests, and challenges.

(**What is being compared:** life before/after having kids; **three clear points of comparison:** new responsibilities, interests, challenges; **opinion:** the change gave life more purpose)

Weak: Married life is very different from being single. Being married changes life in many ways.

(**What is being compared: life** before/after getting married. No clear points of comparison or opinion)

Weak: When people switched from vinyl records to compact discs, it changed the way we listened to music.

vainely

(**What is being compared:** listening to music before/after compact discs. No clear points of comparison or opinion)

Focused Practice

A. Read the following essay assignment. Then work with a partner to decide which kind of background information you might need in an introductory paragraph on this topic. Check (✓) the information you choose.

Compare or contrast life before and after washing machines.

   ✓   **1.** Information about various types of washing machines ✓

         2. Information about various fashion trends

         3. Information about where to buy washers and dryers

   ✓   **4.** Information about various ways of cleaning clothes ✓

B. Read the following essay assignment. Then write a thesis statement in one or two sentences using the information given. Discuss your answers with a partner.

Compare or contrast life before and after a significant invention.

1. Topic (Before/After): Before the arrival of cell phones
   Opinion: Communication was much different when we only had landlines.
   Points of Comparison: Contacting loved ones in an emergency was more challenging, and people had less access to information.

   Communication was much different before cell phones in that contacting loved ones in an emergency was more challenging and people had less access to information. (one sentence) **OR** *Communication was much different when people only had landlines. Before the arrival of cell phones, contacting loved ones in an emergency was more challenging and people had less access to information.* (two sentences)

2. Topic (Before/After): MP3 players ~~melhoria~~
   Opinion: MP3 players are a great improvement over CD players
   Points of Comparison: The MP3 format is much more convenient for listening to music and it is easier to organize your songs.

MP3 players are a great improvement over CD players but with MP3 the people had a format more convenient for listening and they could organize better your songs

3. Topic (Before/After): Texting
   Opinion: Texting has changed the way people interact.
   Points of Comparison: People can communicate faster and more easily, and texting is less intrusive that phone calls.

Texting has changed the way people interact. Now the people get communicate with greater ease and agility

4. Topic (Before/After): Advances in film technology
   Opinion: Movie watching is now more exciting than before.
   Points of Comparison: There is better sound, higher picture quality, and more realistic special effects.

Movie watching is now more exciting, because now there is better sound, higher picture quality and more realistic

C. *Read the introductory paragraph for an essay on the topic in Exercise A. Then answer the questions. Discuss your answers with a partner.*

routine obligation

4 Life was much more difficult before people had basic machines in the home to help them with daily chores. Without the washing machine, doing the laundry was hard work. To avoid doing laundry, people would go weeks or sometimes months before washing their dirty clothes. Early washing machines arrived some time during the nineteenth century, but they still required manual labor. However, once the automatic washer became available in the late 1930s, this dreaded task became much more manageable and even pleasant by comparison. Life has changed dramatically since the invention of the automatic washing machine. Today's method of doing the laundry involves almost no physical labor, takes much less time, and cleans fabrics more effectively.

D le li, olha as palavras

number 4

1. What information from Exercise A did the writer include as background? *ways of cleaning clothes.*

2. What is the writer's thesis statement? Underline it.

3. Will the writer show how life was similar or different before automatic washers? How do you know?

4. What is the writer's opinion about the change that will be discussed in the body of the essay?

5. What three points of comparison do you expect the essay to cover?

Your Own Writing

homework

Finding Out More

A. *You may want to learn more about the invention or event you chose for your compare-contrast essay.*

- Go online or to the library to find out more about what life was like before and after the invention or event. You may want to use the following keywords when you search for information online: *life before (your topic), life after (your topic),* or *"then and now" + (your topic).*

- In addition to looking for information online or at the library, do some research of your own.

  Assignment 1: Interview three people who have experienced the arrival of this significant invention. Ask them to compare and contrast life before and after the invention.

  Assignment 2: Interview three people who experienced this event with you or have experienced a similar kind of event. Ask them to compare and contrast life before and after the event.

B. *Take notes on what you found out. Record key information about what life was like before and after the invention or event, including similarities and differences. Note the sources for your information. Add the information to your T-chart on page 96.*

C. **Checking in.** *Share your information with a partner. Did your partner . . .*

- gather enough information about life before and after the invention or event?

- find at least three points of comparison?

- use at least three reliable sources?

Use this information when you write your essay.

Planning Your Introduction

A. *List the background information you will need to include in your introduction.*

_____

_____

_____

_____

B. *Write a draft of your thesis statement. Make sure your thesis statement includes the topic (e.g., before/after the invention/event) and whether your essay will focus on similarities or differences. Be sure to include the specific points of comparison your essay will discuss. You may also want to include your opinion about the change. Look back at your freewriting and compare-contrast chart to help you.*

_____

_____

C. **Checking in.** *Share your thesis statement with a partner. Did your partner . . .*

- clearly state what will be compared or contrasted (e.g., life before and life after the invention/event)?

- explain whether the essay will present similarities or differences?

- include at least three specific points of comparison about the topic?

D. *Tell your partner what you like about his or her thesis statement. If you have any suggestions for improving it share them. Then tell your partner what kind of supporting evidence you expect to see in his or her essay, based on the thesis statement.*

E. *Based on your partner's feedback, you may want to rewrite your thesis statement.*

■ THE BODY

When you wrote your four-paragraph essay in Unit 2, you used your two body paragraphs to present and develop ideas in support of your thesis statement. In Unit 3, you wrote four or five paragraphs based on the number of solutions you presented. Now you will be writing either a four- or five-paragraph compare-contrast essay, depending on the method you choose.

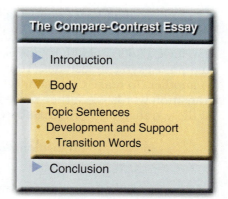

There are two methods for organizing the body paragraphs of a compare-contrast essay. You can use the *block method* or the *point-by-point method*.

In the *block method*, you discuss all the points of comparison about your first topic (e.g., life before the invention or event). Then you discuss the same points of comparison in the same order about your second topic (e.g., life after the invention or event). If you choose the block method for the unit assignment, you will write two body paragraphs; each one will cover three points of comparison.

In the *point-by-point method*, you discuss each point of comparison about the two topics (e.g., life before and after the invention or event) one at a time. If you choose the point-by-point method for the unit assignment, you will write three body paragraphs, one for each of the three points of comparison.

Example:

Thesis Statement: Life before the washing machine was dramatically different from the way it is now. Today's method of doing the laundry involves almost no physical labor, takes much less time, and cleans more effectively.

Block Method	Point-by-Point Method

Body Paragraph 1: Before Automatic Washing Machines
  A. Amount of physical labor
  B. Time required
  C. Effectiveness of the method
 	
Body Paragraph 2: After Automatic Washing Machines
  A. Amount of physical labor
  B. Time required
  C. Effectiveness of the method
	Body Paragraph 1: Amount of Physical Labor
	  A. Before automatic washing machines
	  B. After automatic washing machines
	
	Body Paragraph 2: Time Required
	  A. Before automatic washing machines
	  B. After automatic washing machines
	
	Body Paragraph 3: Effectiveness of the Method
	  A. Before automatic washing machines
	  B. After automatic washing machines

Writing Topic Sentences

As you learned in Units 2 and 3, a body paragraph begins with a topic sentence that clearly states the controlling idea of the paragraph.

You have also learned that topic sentences often begin with listing-order transition words and phrases to connect ideas from one sentence to the next or from one paragraph to another. To make these connections in a compare-contrast essay, writers also use transition words when they present an additional similarity or difference. Some examples of these transition words are shown in the following chart.

Transition Words and Phrases That Show Addition
another Another major improvement in modern films is improved picture quality.
in addition to In addition to better sound and images, films today also have much better special effects.
just as . . . also Just as the Internet has brought the world closer together, it has also made us feel that life is moving much faster.
not only . . . but also The Internet has not only made banking easier, but it has also improved people's access to breaking news.

Writers also use transition words and phrases to show direct contrasts between two people, places, or things, as seen in the following chart.

Transition Words and Phrases That Show Contrast
Between Two Ideas:
unlike / in contrast to Unlike gasoline-powered vehicles, hybrid cars are more environmentally friendly.
however / on the other hand Writing letters by hand feels special and intimate; writing emails, on the other hand, can feel ordinary and impersonal.
while / whereas While some may see the Internet as a huge waste of time, others see it as a productive way to communicate and do business.
Between Two Events:
prior to / before Prior to owning a computer, it was much harder to manage life's daily tasks.
once / when / after Once I owned a computer, my way of doing things improved significantly.

Focused Practice

A. *Look at each pair of topic sentences. Decide whether they would best fit in a block or point-by-point essay. Check (✓) "Block" or "Point-by-Point." Then discuss your answers with a partner.*

1. __✓__ Block   ____ Point-by-Point

   Topic Sentence 1: Not so long ago, when people visited their local bookstore or library, they could enjoy flipping through the pages of various books.

   Topic Sentence 2: However, as soon as e-readers came on the scene, reading became a digital and interactive experience.

2. ____ Block   __✓__ Point-by-Point

   Topic Sentence 1: The Sony Walkman made it possible to listen to music almost anywhere.

   Topic Sentence 2: In addition to making music portable, the Walkman also started a revolution in mobile technology.

3. __✓__ Block   ____ Point-by-Point

   Topic Sentence 1: In the past, people didn't take space travel seriously, considering it only something from science fiction movies.

   Topic Sentence 2: Science fiction or not, when the first man walked on the moon, people gained a new sense of hope and possibility.

4. ____ Block   __✓__ Point-by-Point

   Topic Sentence 1: Once Wi-Fi became available, it made connecting computers to the Internet much less complicated.

   Topic Sentence 2: Wi-Fi not only simplified Internet connectivity, but it also let people surf the Web from almost anywhere.

B. *Read the following thesis statements. Write a topic sentence for each body paragraph, using the transition words and phrases in parentheses. In each topic sentence, rephrase a boldfaced point of comparison from the thesis statement. Two topic sentences are done for you.*

1. **Thesis Statement:** When people switched from home phones to cell phones, they experienced many positive changes. They not only had **more freedom of movement**, but they could also **communicate with others** and **access information more easily**.

Block Organization

   Topic Sentence 1: (**before**) *Before the cell phone, people could only make calls from certain places, and it was also harder to get in touch with others and find information.*

   Topic Sentence 2: (**since**) Now the people can make calls in seconds, the information is more easily

   (continued)

   ✱ Roman doesn't like your first word.

Point-by-Point Organization

Topic Sentence 1: (**unlike**) _Unlike land lines, cell phones allow people to make_

calls from just about anywhere.

Topic Sentence 2: (**in contrast to / another benefit**) _____

_____

Topic Sentence 3: (**not only . . . but also**) _____

_____

2. **Thesis Statement:** MP3s files have improved the way people listen to music,
especially when compared to compact discs. MP3 files and compact discs differ in
terms of **the amount of care they require, ease of organization, and access to
new kinds of music.**

Block Organization

Topic Sentence 1: (**prior to**) _Prior to computer MP3 access to_

new kind of music

Topic Sentence 2: (**once**)

Once I discovere a new way to

save my songs

Point-by-Point Organization

Topic Sentence 1: (**first**) _First the MP3 improve the_

way easier than before to listen music.

Topic Sentence 2: (**in addition to / another improvement**) _In addition_

MP3 transformer the way to listen music

Topic Sentence 3: (**just as . . . also**) _Also MP3 did music_

easier and organization.

Block/ time

Point by Point

Developing a Body Paragraph

In Unit 2, you learned that the remaining sentences in a body paragraph develop and support the controlling idea in the topic sentence. When you develop your ideas in a compare-contrast essay, you explain and/or describe how two people, things, or ideas are similar and/or are different. Then you support each idea with facts, examples, and/or anecdotes.

Focused Practice

A. *On page 99, you read an introductory paragraph for a compare-contrast essay about life before and after the arrival of the washing machine. Read the writer's thesis statement and the first body paragraph. Discuss the questions with a partner.*

Example:

Thesis Statement: Life has changed dramatically since the invention of the automatic washing machine. Today's method of doing the laundry involves almost no physical labor, takes much less time, and cleans fabrics more effectively.

> Before the automatic washer was invented, doing the laundry was physically demanding work. At first, people washed clothes in a local river and rubbed the clothes against rocks. Later, they carried large, heavy buckets of water home to wash the clothes. It was truly back-breaking work. Washerwomen filled large pots with water, heated the water, and scrubbed the clothes with their bare hands against a metal washboard to get out tough stains. Even though they used soap, it took a lot of rubbing and wringing to clean and rinse the clothes. This made their hands sore and damaged their skin. With washing machines, people are no longer subjected to such difficult manual labor. Thanks to indoor plumbing, they do not have to carry gallons of water into their homes anymore. Instead of hurting their backs or hands, people rely on the power and strength of the machine to remove dirt. They don't experience the same soreness and exhaustion that they did when washing clothes by hand.

1. What is the topic sentence? Underline it.

2. What point of comparison does the paragraph present in the topic sentence? Circle the transition word the writer uses to show contrast.

3. How did the automatic washer change the physical act of doing laundry? Identify three supporting details that show what the experience was like . . .

    a. before automatic washing machines.

    b. after automatic washing machines.

B. *Work with a partner. Read body paragraph. Then choose the two supporting details that best complete it. Write them on the appropriate lines.*

> Prior to the invention of the automatic washing machine, doing the wash was an all-day event. First, the water buckets had to be filled and sometimes carried quite a distance. _D_____
> I remember my grandmother telling me about how she would spend an entire day washing the family's clothes and sheets by hand. When it was a washing day, no other chores could get done. Now, people can get a single load of laundry washed in less than half an hour. They can even select short cycles to make the process go faster. _And C analists the give alone._____
> She could forget about the washing and do other chores around the house, or even read or rest for a few minutes. That would never have been possible without her automatic washer.

a. When there were many clothes to wash, the process could easily last more than one day, so clothes weren't washed that often.

b. Special laundry detergents have made clothes come out much cleaner than they did when my grandmother was around.

c. After my grandmother got her first automatic washer, she was delighted at how much time it saved her.

d. Then each piece of clothing had to be cleaned, rinsed, and squeezed individually.

C. *Read the incomplete paragraph from the body of a point-by-point compare-contrast essay. Add three supporting details to complete the body paragraph. Consider including facts, examples, or anecdotes as support. Discuss your completed paragraph with a partner.*

> Before the cell phone, people did not have to worry about being constantly distracted by calls. There would be a message on the answering machine waiting for them. People could focus on what they were doing and where they were. While driving, people took pleasure in seeing how neighborhoods and landscapes changed from one place to another. When they went to lunch with a friend, they enjoyed spending time talking together. Today, however, people can never really escape the call of the cell phone. _they people use message._
> _they use more messages than call. life._
> _more._

Your Own Writing

Planning Your Body Paragraphs

A. *Before you begin writing your body paragraphs, complete one of the following outlines. Copy your thesis statement from page 100.*

- Review the two ways to organize a compare-contrast essay on page 101.
- Select the method and number of paragraphs best suited to your topic. If you want to experiment with more than one method of organization, complete both outlines.

Compare-Contrast Essay

▶ Thesis Statement: _Difference between Red and White_

Block Method

▶ Body Paragraph 1

▶ Topic Sentence: _It's important choose a color_

  ▶ Point of Comparison 1 _White is more important_

    ▶ Supporting Details:

    - _the flag of peace is this color_
    - _many culture accept this color like peace_
    - _____

  ▶ Point of Comparison 2 _Love's color_

    ▶ Supporting Details:

    - _Many people association with Love_
    - _Some people doesn't like_
    - _association with hot color_

  ▶ Point of Comparison 3 _Mix this color is my favorite color_

    ▶ Supporting Details:

    - _____
    - _____
    - _____

▶ Body Paragraph 2

▶ Topic Sentence: _____

    ▶ Point of Comparison 1 _____

        ▶ Supporting Details:

            • _____

            • _____

            • _____

    ▶ Point of Comparison 2 _____

        ▶ Supporting Details:

            • _____

            • _____

            • _____

    ▶ Point of Comparison 3 _____

        ▶ Supporting Details:

            • _____

            • _____

            • _____

Point-by-Point

▶ Body Paragraph 1

▶ Topic Sentence: _____

    ▶ Point of Comparison 1 _____

        ▶ Supporting Details:

            • _____

            • _____

            • _____

▶ Body Paragraph 2 *Conclusion*

▶ Topic Sentence: _____

   ▶ Point of Comparison 2 _____

      ▶ Supporting Details:

         • _____

         • _____

         • _____

▶ Body Paragraph 3

▶ Topic Sentence: _____

   ▶ Point of Comparison 1 _____

      ▶ Supporting Details:

         • _____

         • _____

         • _____

B. Checking in. *Share your outline with a partner. Did your partner . . .*

   • choose the method that will work best for his or her essay, block or point-by point?

   • order the points of comparison appropriately, if he or she is using the point-by-point method?

   • provide interesting supporting details?

C. *Based on your partner's feedback, you may want to rewrite parts of your outline.*

■ THE CONCLUSION

As you have learned in previous units, your concluding paragraph brings your essay to a close. Some writers include transition phrases, such as *In conclusion, To sum up, In sum*, or *In summary* to let readers know that the conclusion is beginning. Other writers leave these phrases out. The choice is yours.

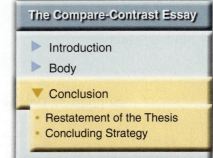

In a compare-contrast essay, the conclusion should return to the controlling idea presented in the thesis statement. You may also offer a final comment about the purpose of the comparison; that is, why it is important or helpful for people to think about the similarities or differences you have discussed. For example, you wouldn't write about life before and after the Internet just to analyze the differences; you also need to say why it is useful for people to see the differences.

Here are two concluding strategies you might want to use to end your compare-contrast essay about before and after an important invention or event:

1. Offer an interesting observation about why life in the past was better or worse.

2. Suggest how the comparison is relevant to people's lives today or in the future.

Focused Practice

Read the model of a concluding paragraph, and answer the questions on page 111.

To sum up, life has greatly improved since the arrival of the automatic washing machine. Whereas in the past, people spent a great deal of time and effort on a single load of laundry, today they can simply throw their clothes into the machine and read a book or have a cup of tea. Recently, I have heard that some people are going back to hand washing because it's more natural and better for the environment. Others just value the "good old days" and want to keep the tradition alive. I doubt that most people will ever part with their automatic washing machines, though. Many of us still dread doing the laundry. As my grandmother has said, sometimes change is good.

1. Underline the sentence(s) that restates the thesis statement.

2. What transition words does the writer use to signal that this is the conclusion?

   Sum up

3. What strategy (or strategies) does the writer use to close the essay?

   As my grandmother,

Your Own Writing

Planning Your Conclusion

A. *How will you rephrase your thesis statement in the conclusion? List your ideas here.*

_____

_____

B. *What strategy will you use to close the essay?*

_____

_____

C. **Checking in.** *Share your ideas with a partner. Did your partner . . .*

- discover a new and interesting way to phrase the thesis statement?
- choose an effective concluding strategy?

Writing Your First Draft

A. *Read the* Tip for Writers. *Review your notes on pages 96, 100, and 107–109. Then write the first draft of your essay. When you are finished, give your paragraph a working title. Hand in your draft to your teacher.*

Tip for Writers

When you write your first draft, **consider the style of language** you want for your essay. When writing about facts or providing examples, your style may be more formal. If you have included anecdotes, the language may be less formal.

Revising your work is an essential part of the writing process. This is your opportunity to be sure that your essay has all the important pieces and that it is clear.

Focused Practice

A. *You have read parts of this compare-contrast essay already. Now read and the entire essay to see how the parts fit together.*

Washing Clothes: Then and Now

Life was much more difficult before people had basic machines in the home to help them with daily chores. Without the washing machine, doing the laundry was hard work. To avoid doing the laundry, people would go weeks or sometimes months before washing their dirty clothes. Early washing machines arrived some time during the nineteenth century, but they still required manual labor. However, once the automatic washer became available in the late 1930s, this dreaded task became much more manageable and even pleasant by comparison. Life has changed dramatically since the invention of the automatic washing machine. Today, doing the laundry involves almost no physical labor, takes much less time, and cleans fabrics more effectively.

Before the automatic washer was invented, doing the laundry was physically demanding work. At first, people washed clothes in a local river and rubbed the clothes against rocks. Later, they carried large, heavy buckets of water home to wash the clothes. It was truly back-breaking work. Washerwomen filled large pots with water, heated the water, and scrubbed the clothes with their bare hands against a metal washboard to get out tough stains. Even though they used soap, it took a lot of rubbing and wringing to clean and rinse the clothes. This made their hands sore and damaged their skin. With washing machines, people are no longer subjected to such difficult manual labor. Thanks to indoor plumbing, they do not have to carry gallons of water into their homes anymore. Instead of hurting their backs or hands, people rely on the power and strength of the machine to remove dirt. They don't experience the same soreness and exhaustion that hand washers once did.

Prior to the invention of the automatic washing machine, doing the wash was an all-day event. First, the water buckets had to be filled and sometimes carried quite a distance. Then each piece of clothing had to be cleaned, rinsed, and

(continued)

---

squeezed individually. I remember my grandmother, who often talked about how she would spend an entire day washing the family's clothes and sheets by hand. When it was a washing day, no other chores could get done. Now, people can get a single load of laundry washed in less than half an hour. They can even select short cycles to make the process go faster. After my grandmother got her first automatic washer, she was delighted at how much time it saved her. She could forget about the washing and do other chores around the house, or even read or rest for a few minutes. That would never have been possible without her automatic washer.

Not only does the automatic washing machine help people save time and effort but it also allows them to clean their clothes better. In the past, people had only simple soaps that were rough on their hands and didn't clean very well. To remove excess dirt, they often had to beat clothes against large rocks before rubbing them against the washboard. Because clothes took such a beating, they looked old and worn out very quickly. In contrast, the automatic washer does a terrific job taking out stains. Prewash cycles give dirty clothes an extra cleaning. There are also stronger cycles for heavily soiled clothes and gentle cycles for more delicate fabrics like wool. Thanks to these machines, and better stain-lifting detergents, clothes come out looking super clean and stay looking like new for a much longer time.

To sum up, life has greatly improved since the arrival of the automatic washing machine. Whereas in the past, people spent a great deal of time and effort on a single load of laundry, today they can simply throw their clothes into the machine and read a book or have a cup of tea. Recently, I have heard that some people are going back to hand washing because it's more natural and better for the environment. Others just value the "good old days" and want to keep the tradition alive. I doubt that most people will ever part with their automatic washing machines, though. Many of us still dread doing the laundry. As my grandmother has said, sometimes change is good.

B. *Work with a partner. Answer the questions about the essay.*

1. What is the thesis statement? Underline it.

2. Is the writer comparing or contrasting? How do you know?

3. What is the main point of comparison in paragraph 2? Underline the sentence that states it.

(continued)

4. What is the main point of comparison in paragraph 3? Underline the sentence that states it.

5. What is the main point of comparison in paragraph 4? Underline the sentence that states it.

6. What transition words and phrases in the topic sentences connect the parts of the essay together? Circle them.

7. What facts, examples, anecdotes, or other details support and develop the controlling idea in each body paragraph? Check (✔) three kinds of support and development in each paragraph.

C. Checking in. *Discuss your marked-up essay with another pair of students. Then in your group, share one thing about the essay that you found the most interesting. Explain your answer.*

Building Word Knowledge

Using New Words. The writer used "new words," including old words with new meanings that were used after the arrival of the automatic washing machine, such as *load, cycle, prewash,* and *stain-lifting.*

Work with a partner. Read the words in the chart. Write two definitions for each word to show what it meant before and after the arrival of the computer. Use a dictionary.

	Before Computers	After Computers
1. mouse	a small animal that lives in people's houses or in fields	
2. virus		
3. menu		
4. keys		
5. drive		

Your Own Writing

Revising Your Draft

A. *Read the first draft of your essay. Use the Revision Checklist to identify parts of your writing that might need improvement.*

B. *Review your plans and notes and your responses to the Revision Checklist. Then revise your first draft. Save your revised essay. You will look at it again in the next section.*

Revision Checklist

Did you . . .

☐ express the controlling idea of the essay in your thesis statement?

☐ give enough background in your introduction?

☐ organize your body paragraphs correctly according to block or point-by-point organization?

☐ introduce the comparisons in your body paragraphs with clear topic sentences?

☐ give enough facts, examples, anecdotes, and other details to support and develop your controlling ideas?

☐ restate the controlling idea of the essay in your conclusion?

☐ use an effective concluding strategy?

☐ connect the parts of your essay with transition words and phrases?

☐ use any "new words" in your essay?

☐ use an appropriate style of language in your essay?

☐ give your essay an interesting title?

■ GRAMMAR PRESENTATION

Before you hand in your revised essay, you must check it for any errors in grammar, punctuation, and spelling. In this section, you will learn about adjective clauses. You will focus on this grammar when you edit and proofread your essay.

Adjective Clauses

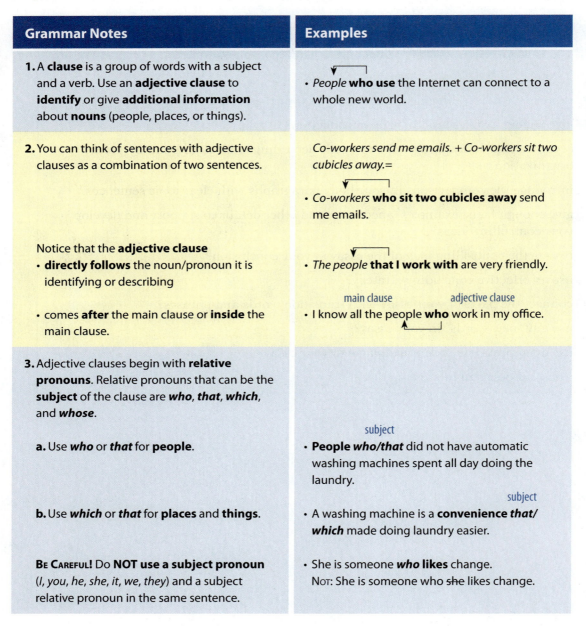

Grammar Notes	Examples
1. A **clause** is a group of words with a subject and a verb. Use an **adjective clause** to **identify** or give **additional information** about **nouns** (people, places, or things).	• *People* **who use** the Internet can connect to a whole new world.
2. You can think of sentences with adjective clauses as a combination of two sentences.	*Co-workers send me emails. + Co-workers sit two cubicles away.=* • *Co-workers* **who sit two cubicles away** send me emails.
Notice that the **adjective clause** • **directly follows** the noun/pronoun it is identifying or describing • comes **after** the main clause or **inside** the main clause.	• *The people* **that I work with** are very friendly. main clause adjective clause • I know all the people **who** work in my office.
3. Adjective clauses begin with **relative pronouns**. Relative pronouns that can be the **subject** of the clause are *who*, *that*, *which*, and *whose*.	
a. Use *who* or *that* for **people**.	subject • **People** *who/that* did not have automatic washing machines spent all day doing the laundry.
b. Use *which* or *that* for **places** and **things**.	subject • A washing machine is a **convenience** *that/which* made doing laundry easier.
Be Careful! Do **NOT** use a subject pronoun (*I, you, he, she, it, we, they*) and a subject relative pronoun in the same sentence.	• She is someone *who* **likes** change. Not: She is someone who ~~she~~ likes change.

4. Some **relative pronouns** (*who(m)*), *that*, *which*, and *whose*) can also be the object of an adjective clause.

a. Use **whom**, **who**, or **that** for **people**. Note that in this case you can also leave out the relative pronoun.

Usage Note: **Whom** is very formal and may be used in writing. Most people do not use **whom** in everyday speech. **That** is less formal than **who**. In everyday speech, most people use no relative pronoun.

Formality
more

- I enjoy communicating with the

  object   subject

  people **whom** I have met on the Internet.
- I enjoy communicating with the people **who I have met** on the Internet.
- I enjoy communicating with the people **that I have met** on the Internet.
- I enjoy communicating with the people I **met** on the Internet.

less

Formality
more

b. Use **which** or **that** for **things**. You can also leave out the relative pronoun.

Usage Note: Again, **that** is less formal than **which**. In everyday speech, most people use no relative pronoun. In writing, use either.

- I have the information **which I need** at my fingertips.
- I have the information **that I need** at my fingertips.
- I have the information **I need** at my fingertips.

less

5. There are two kinds of adjective clauses, **identifying** and **nonidentifying**.

a. An **identifying** adjective clause **is necessary** to identify the noun it refers to.

- Internet connections **that send out wireless signals** are available in many airports.
  (*The adjective clause is necessary to identify the type of Internet signals.*)

b. A **nonidentifying** adjective clause gives **additional information** about the noun it refers to. It is not necessary to identify the noun. The noun is often already identified with an adjective such as *first*, *last*, *best*, or *most*, or is the name of a specific person or place.

- My *first* computer, **which I bought ten years ago**, doesn't have Wi-Fi capability.
  (*The adjective clause gives additional information but it isn't needed to identify the computer. The computer has already been identified as the speaker's first.*)

Usage Note: In writing, use **commas** to separate nonidentifying adjective clauses from the rest of the sentence.

- Unlike my kids, **who don't think twice about using new technology,** I have a love-hate relationship with it.

Be Careful! Do **NOT use** *that* to introduce nonidentifying adjective clauses. Use **who** for people or **which** for places and things.

- Debit cards, **which link directly to your bank account**, are a lot more convenient than cash.
  Not: Debit cards, ~~that~~ link directly to your bank account, are a lot more convenient than cash.

Focused Practice

A. *Underline the adjective clause in each sentence. Add commas when needed.*

1. A smartphone is a device <u>that allows people to make calls, text, and browse the Web</u>.

2. LCD televisions, <u>which consume a lot less energy,</u> are better for the environment.

3. In the past, people only had soaps <u>that were hard on the hands</u>.

4. A curmudgeon is an old person <u>who is often angry and annoyed</u>.

5. The microwave, <u>which has revolutionized food preparation,</u> saves people a lot of time.

6. People don't experience the same physical exhaustion <u>that they did when washing clothes by hand</u>.

7. Many people <u>who think about changing careers</u> are worried about the risks.

8. She is searching for a career <u>that will give her the financial freedom that she has always wanted</u>.

9. Today's televisions, <u>which are slimmer and lighter,</u> take up less space than the older models.

10. Greater convenience is a benefit <u>that comes from using mobile devices</u>.

B. *Combine the sentences to take out unnecessary repetition. Make at least one adjective clause. In some cases, more than one answer is possible. The first one is done for you.*

1. Few people would give up their cell phones.
   I know these people.

   Few people that/whom I know would give up their cell phones.

2. The automobile was an invention.
   The automobile changed the way people lived and traveled.

   _____

   _____

3. I don't always agree with my grandparents.
   My grandparents often long for the good old days.

   _____

   _____

4. The iPhone® is one of the most popular smartphones today.
   The iPhone was developed by Apple Inc.

   _____

   _____

5. Reaching the top of Mount Everest was a life-changing moment.
I will never forget that event.

_____

_____

6. MP3 players allow people to save songs to their computer.
MP3 players use digital technology.

_____

_____

7. Modern films use special effects.
The effects make movies seem much more realistic.

_____

_____

8. Having children is an experience.
This experience gives people a new purpose in life.

_____

_____

9. My sister enjoys reading books on her e-reader.
My sister travels a lot for work.

_____

_____

10. I grew up in the 1970s.
The 1970s was a time when people lived happily without cell phones.

_____

_____

C. *Complete the adjective clauses in your own words. Discuss your answers with a partner.*

1. I would love to create a new invention *that* _____.

2. My best friend is a person *who* _____.

3. People *who* _____

can experience eye strain and headaches.

4. I have always wanted a cell phone *that* _____.

(continued)

5. Some experts predict that one day people will be able to buy a computer *which*

_____.

6. Televisions *that* _____

are almost always more expensive.

7. Her grandparents come from an older generation of people *who*

_____.

8. Cell phones *which* _____

have made finding information online much easier.

D. *Read and edit the paragraph. There are nine errors in the use of adjective clauses. The first error has already been corrected for you. Find and correct eight more.*

> Alexander Graham Bell, who invented the telephone, lived from 1847 to 1922.
> Bell grew up in Scotland, where he lived with his mother, father, and two brothers.
> His father, that was a university professor, wrote a number of books that focused
> on speech production for the deaf. Bell's early interest in sound also came from
> his mother who started to go deaf while Bell was still a young boy. At school,
> Bell studied music and speech and later became a teacher. He eventually moved
> to the United States and started his own school in Boston, Massachusetts, for
> people, who were deaf or hearing disabled. During this time, Bell was also doing
> experiments who combined sound and electricity. Finally, Bell, whom had worked
> tirelessly on his invention, made his first successful telephone call on March 10,
> 1876. Some people believed the invention would never become popular who
> criticized Bell. In time, however, Bell's telephone became a standard feature in
> American homes, and the Bell Telephone Company, that he started a year after that
> famous first call, was very successful in the years that they followed.

E. *Write five sentences related to the assignment you chose on page 99. Use adjective clauses. These may be sentences you already have in your essay.*

1. _____

   _____

2. _____

   _____

3. _____

   _____

4. _____

   _____

5. _____

   _____

Your Own Writing

Editing Your Draft

A. *Use the Editing Checklist to edit and proofread your essay.*

B. *Prepare a clean copy of the final draft of your essay and hand it in to your teacher.*

Editing Checklist
Did you . . .
☐ include adjective clauses and use them correctly?
☐ use correct verb forms, punctuation, and spelling?
☐ use "new words" and other words correctly?

UNIT 5 Happiness

IN THIS UNIT You will be writing an essay about the causes and effects of happiness or stress in everyday life.

You may have heard that wine and cheese improve with age. But what about people? Does life get better as we get older? Do people become more or less happy as they age? Research has begun to look more closely at the relationship between age and happiness, and the findings may be surprising. Do you think you will be happier in twenty years than you are today?

Planning for Writing

■ BRAINSTORM

A. *Did you experience any of the following feelings during a large part of the day yesterday? Check one or two that apply.*

☒ anger	_____ happiness	☒ stress
_____ enjoyment	☒ sadness	☒ worry

B. Using a Cause-Effect Web. When you think about a topic, you can use a cause-effect web to show the relationship between why a situation or event occurs and what happens as a result of it. Use arrows to the topic oval for causes, and arrows from the topic oval for effects.

Complete the cause-effect web. Put the emotion you experienced the most yesterday in the center oval. Then fill in some of the causes (sources) and effects (results) of that emotion. Add ovals if needed.

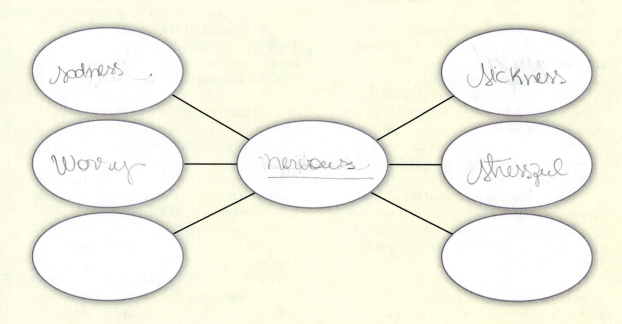

C. *Consider what is happening in the average person's life at the ages of 18, 50, and 85. Write about what age you think a person is usually happier and why. Discuss your ideas with the class.*

18 about happiness a new life, adult life. Indepent life

50 relaxing because now then retired finacial more relax

85 Relax enjoy your retired loke care Grandchild
and thace more

123

The New York Times   May 31, 2010

Happiness May Come with Age   By NICHOLAS BAKALAR

1   It is inevitable.[1] The muscles weaken. Hearing and vision fade. We get wrinkled and stooped.[2] We can't run, or even walk, as fast as we used to. We have aches and pains in parts of our bodies we never even noticed before. We get old.

2   It sounds miserable, but apparently it is not. A large Gallup poll has found that by almost any measure, people get happier as they get older, and researchers are not sure why.

3   "It could be that there are environmental changes," said Arthur A. Stone, the lead author of a new study based on the survey, "or it could be psychological changes about the way we view the world, or it could even be biological—for example brain chemistry or endocrine[3] changes."

4   The telephone survey, carried out in 2008, covered more than 340,000 people nationwide, ages 18 to 85, asking various questions about age and sex, current events, personal finances, health, and other matters.

5   The survey also asked about "global well-being" by having each person rank overall life satisfaction on a 10–point scale, an assessment many people may make from time to time, if not in a strictly formalized way.

6   Finally, there were six yes-or-no questions: Did you experience the following feelings during a large part of the day yesterday: enjoyment, happiness, stress, worry, anger, sadness. The answers, the researchers say, reveal "hedonic well-being," a person's immediate experience of those psychological states, [. . .].

7   The results, published online May 17 in the *Proceedings of the National Academy of Sciences*, were good news for old people, and for those who are getting old. On the global measure, people start out at age 18 feeling pretty good about themselves, and then, apparently, life begins to throw curve balls. They feel worse and worse until they hit 50. At that point, there is a sharp reversal, and people keep getting happier as they age. By the time they are 85, they are even more satisfied with themselves than they were at 18.

8   In measuring immediate well-being— yesterday's emotional state—the researchers found that stress declines from age 22 onward, reaching its lowest point at 85. Worry stays fairly steady until 50, then sharply drops off. Anger decreases steadily from 18 on, and sadness rises to a peak at 50, declines to 73, then rises slightly again to 85. Enjoyment and happiness have similar curves: they both decrease gradually until we hit 50, rise steadily for the next 25 years, and then decline very slightly at the end, but they never again reach the low point of our early 50s.

9   Other experts were impressed with the work. Andrew J. Oswald, a professor of psychology at Warwick Business School in England, who has published several studies on human happiness, called the findings important and, in some ways, heartening.[4] "It's a very encouraging fact that we can expect to be happier in our early 80s than we were in our 20s," he said. "And it's not being driven predominantly[5] by things that happen in life. It's something very deep and quite human that seems to be driving this."

10   Dr. Stone, who is a professor of psychology at the State University of New York at Stony Brook,

---

[1] **inevitable:** certain to happen, impossible to avoid

[2] **stooped:** standing with your back and shoulders bent forward

[3] **endocrine:** relating to the hormones in your blood

[4] **heartening:** making someone feel happier and more hopeful

[5] **predominantly:** mostly, mainly

said that the findings raised questions that needed more study. "These results say there are distinctive patterns here," he said, "and it's worth some research effort to try to figure out what's going on. Why at age 50 does something seem to start to change?"

11 The study was not designed to figure out which factors make people happy, and the poll's health questions were not specific enough to draw any conclusions about the effect of disease or disability on happiness in old age. But the researchers did look at four possibilities: the sex of the interviewee, whether the person had a partner, whether there were children at home and employment status. "These are four reasonable candidates," Dr. Stone said, "but they don't make much difference."

12 For people under 50 who may sometimes feel gloomy, there may be consolation[6] here. The view seems a bit bleak[7] right now, but look at the bright side: you are getting old.

---

[6] **consolation:** something that makes you feel better when you are sad or disappointed
[7] **bleak:** without anything to make you feel cheerful or hopeful

Building Word Knowledge

Using Reporting Verbs. Reporting verbs are used when you want to say what someone's exact words are or when you want to communicate someone else's idea in your own words. The most common reporting verb is *say*. *Said* is used to report what someone said in the past.

Examples:

My father always **says**, "Life starts at 60." (My father still says it from time to time.)

My father always **says** that life really begins when you turn 60. (These are my words to tell what my father usually says).

My father always **said**, "Life starts at 60." (My father used to say it, but he no longer does.)

My father always **said** that life really begins when you turn 60. (These are my words to tell what my father usually said, but he no longer does).

Say and *said* *are used several times in the reading on page 124. Circle them and notice how they are used. Then underline the other verbs in the same sentences. Notice the verb forms that the writer uses. Are they present or past?*

Focused Practice

A. *Reread the article on page 124. Decide whether each statement is true (T) or false (F). Then write the paragraph number(s) to show where you found support for your answer.*

_____ **1.** The writer states that everyone ages. Paragraph _____

_____ **2.** Researchers understand why people get happier as they get older. Paragraph _____

_____ **3.** Dr. Stone believes strongly that people get happier because of environmental,

psychological, and biological changes. Paragraph _____

(continued)

I thought "the life is better after 25 old" this are my world before 25 year old
My mother always said " go out and enjoy weather"
My mother used to say, and still say.

_____ **4.** Gallup (the research company) polled only 18- to 85-year-olds by phone.

Paragraph _____

_____ **5.** People are usually happiest around age 50. Paragraph _____

_____ **6.** Professor Oswald is optimistic about the findings of this study. Paragraph _____

_____ **7.** Dr. Stone thinks that more research is needed on this topic. Paragraph _____

_____ **8.** The goal of this study was to find out what makes people happy. Paragraph _____

_____ **9.** Dr. Stone believes that one's sex, being in a relationship, having children at

home, and one's employment status make a difference in one's happiness.

Paragraph _____

B. *In baseball, a pitcher sometimes throws a "curve ball" so the batter will have a hard time predicting where the ball will go. The writer uses this curve ball metaphor in his article. Read paragraph 7 again. Then discuss your ideas with a partner. Write one or two sentences that explain what the author says happens to people around age 18.*

In the age 18 people are very intressful
about feature and adult life. By the
time people are 85 age are more
relocing with your choice and
life.

_____

C. *Read the* Tip for Writers *and reread the article on page 124. List the names of the sources the writer uses. Then work with a partner. Discuss why these sources might be considered reliable for this article.*

Dr Stone who is a professor of
psychology at the state University
of NY

_____

_____

Tip for Writers

In academic writing it is important to **use information from trustworthy, reliable sources to support your ideas**. In "Happiness May Come with Age," Nicholas Bakalar uses quotations from experts on aging and happiness. Quotations, also called direct speech, are the speaker's exact words.

D. *Why do you think people seem to get happier as they get older? Complete this part of a cause-effect web. In the center oval write: "People get happier as they age." Fill in the outer ovals with three or four causes.*

good job

emotion
grow up

People get happier as they age

start family

good
financial
economic +

E. *Look at your cause-effect web in Exercise D. Write a paragraph about why you think people get happier as they age.*

People think get happier as they age. People think When I catch up this age they will be happy. However, the happiness is independ age. Its more feelings. So, People think when catch up a family, good job, emotion establish they Will be happy. they need to know to be happy with yourself. then, These people can will be happy with world

Writing a Cause-Effect Essay

In this unit you are going to write a cause-effect essay about happiness or stress in daily life. A cause-effect essay shows why or how something happened (the causes) and the results of that situation or event (the effects). The focus of your essay will be on either the causes or the effects, not both.

Like all essays, a cause-effect essay contains three parts.

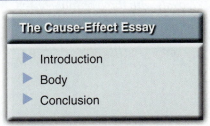

The Cause-Effect Essay

▶ Introduction
▶ Body
▶ Conclusion

Step 1   Prewriting

For a cause-effect essay, the first prewriting step is to select a topic that has clear causes and effects. You must also decide whether you want your essay to focus on causes or on effects. It is important to remember that a situation or event will usually have more than one cause and more than one effect.

You can ask yourself several questions. *What happened? What factors caused that situation or event to happen? What were the effects or results of that situation or event?* For example, if your topic is explaining the relationship between happiness and aging, you might ask yourself: *What happens as people age? Do they become happier? If so, what are some specific factors that cause this? What are the results of people becoming happier as they age?*

Your Own Writing

Choosing Your Assignment

A. *Choose Assignment 1 or Assignment 2.*

1. What are some primary causes or effects of happiness in everyday life? Write about the causes or effects of happiness. Include two or three causes or effects of happiness.

2. What are the major causes or effects of stress in everyday life? Write about the causes or the effects of stress. Include two or three causes or effects of stress.

B. *Freewrite for ten minutes on your assignment. Here are some questions to get you started:*

- Why is this assignment interesting to you? *Because I understand this topic*
- What do you already know about happiness and stress in everyday life? *Work/*
- What makes you and the people you know happy or stressed? *good/family*
- What do you want to find out more about before you write your essay? *Information*

C. Checking in. *Work with a partner who chose the same assignment. Discuss the ideas and details you wrote in Exercise B. Did your partner . . .*

- focus on either the causes or effects of happiness or stress?
- clearly identify two or three causes or effects of happiness or stress?

Share your ideas about your partner's topic. Based on your discussion, make changes and additions to your writing.

D. *Complete the cause-effect web. Organize your ideas to show the causes and effects of either happiness or stress. Start by writing "Happiness" or "Stress" in the center oval. Fill in as much information as you can. You will have a chance to review, change, or add to the information later in the unit.*

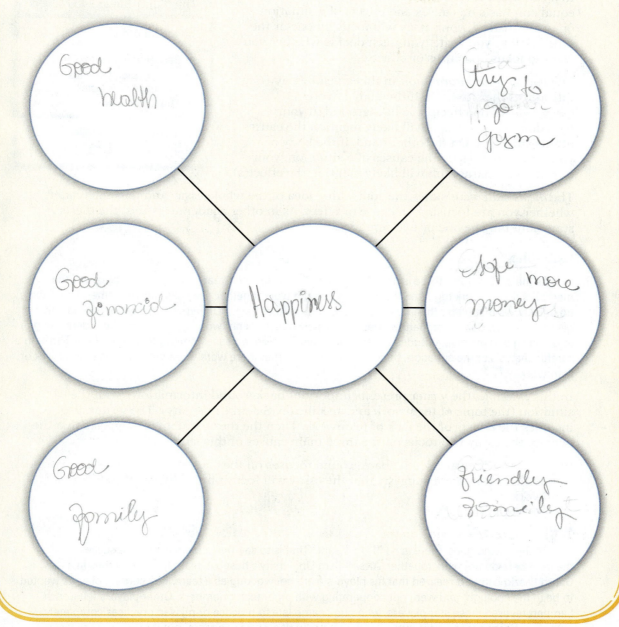

Good health

try to go gym

Good financial

Happiness

dope more money

Good family

friendly family

② People are more stressful today because the life running. They are more multitosking than before. Usually Women didn't work out. the mon just be a "mother". The world change. the people wait more and change more each other.

■ THE INTRODUCTION

In a cause-effect essay, you will usually not write with equal emphasis on causes and effects of a situation or event. Instead, your essay will focus on one or the other. Before you write, you must decide whether you want to focus on causes or effects.

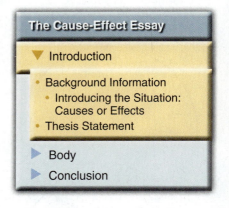

The *background information* in this type of essay introduces the situation. If the body of your essay focuses on effects, the background in your introductory paragraph will likely mention the causes of this situation. On the other hand, if the body of your essay focuses on the causes of a situation, your introductory paragraph will likely mention the effect(s).

The *thesis statement* states the controlling idea of the whole essay and tells the reader whether you are focusing on cause or effect. As in other academic essays, the thesis statement may be one or two sentences.

Example:

As the saying goes, there is no "I" in "team." That is to say, a team cannot be successful if the members do not work together. If teammates do not work together, they cannot win games. These days no one knows that better than Coach Laszlo Lambert. After Salem University's baseball team lost five games in a row, Coach Lambert realized that his players were not working as a team. Confidence began to diminish and positive attitudes became negative. Tension increased among team members. Through a careful analysis of the situation, the coach determined that there were three main causes of their lack of teamwork.

In this example, the writer presents important background information about the situation (the topic of teamwork and specifically Salem University). The writer also includes the effects of the lack of teamwork. Then the thesis statement suggests that the body of the essay will focus on the three main causes of this situation.

In the following example, the background focuses on the causes of the lack of teamwork so the thesis statement suggests that the essay will focus on the effects of the lack of teamwork.

Example:

As the saying goes, there is no "I" in "team." That is to say that a team cannot be successful if the members do not work together. After Salem University's baseball team lost five games in a row, Coach Laszlo Lambert realized that his players were not working as a team. Key starting players wanted to be in the spotlight and were not cooperating with other team members. Other players felt Coach Lambert favored these star players, who often came late to practice or missed practices completely, with no consequences. There was also an unhealthy rivalry among team members who were jealous of each other's talents. Through a careful analysis of the situation, Lambert determined that this lack of teamwork was strongly affecting the team's success in several significant ways.

Focused Practice

A. *Decide whether the following ideas are causes or effects of depression. Write* C *for Cause or* E *for Effect. Then discuss your answers with the class.*

_C_ **1.** abuse or emotional trauma

_E_ **2.** avoiding social interaction

_E_ **3.** change in weight

_C_ **4.** death of a loved one

_C_ **5.** difficulty getting out of bed

_E_ **6.** inability to sleep

____ **7.** lack of interest in daily activities

_C_ **8.** major life changes

_C_ **9.** personal conflicts with family or friends

_E_ **10.** serious illness

B. *Read the following essay assignment and thesis statements. Then decide which thesis statement is for an essay that focuses on causes and which thesis statement is for an essay that focuses on effects. Write* C *for Cause or* E *for Effect.*

Write about the causes or effects of depression.

____ **1.** We need to watch out for certain signs of depression so that we can help those who may be suffering from it.

____ **2.** There are several reasons why a person might suddenly become depressed.

____ **3.** It is extremely important to understand where depression comes from so that we can help those who are suffering from it.

____ **4.** According to recent studies, depression can change a person's behavior in three major areas.

____ **5.** Mood swings, excessive irritability, and overeating can all be signs that a person is suffering from depression.

____ **6.** A career change or move to a different city could certainly be considered reasons why a person suddenly becomes depressed.

C. *Read the following essay assignment and the introductory paragraph. Choose the thesis that best completes the paragraph or write your own thesis statement. Then discuss your choice with a partner.*

What do you think causes people to become happier as they get older?

The results of a recent Gallup poll described in the *New York Times* may change people's attitude towards the inevitable—getting old. These results are significant considering our current attitudes about aging. In our culture we seem to value being young—or at least keeping our bodies looking that way. We see television ads for exercise equipment and anti-aging creams that promise to take years off our appearance and make us feel younger. We are told to join a gym because, if we look young and strong on the outside, we will be happy on the inside. The assumption is that "youth equals happiness" and "aging equals unhappiness." We ignore evidence that suggests that the opposite is true: aging can bring happiness and the effects are real. No one seems to notice the radiant, satisfied smile of a grandmother enjoying her favorite activities, such as playing with her grandchildren or working in her garden. Who really pays attention to a group of worry-free, gray-haired old men sitting together, trading stories or playing cards? People automatically seem to believe that being younger means being happier. However, the results of a Gallup poll clearly contradict this view. The reality, according to the poll, is that people seem to get happier as they get older.

_____

_____

1. Although the poll did not explain why this is true, I think there are three likely causes of this phenomenon.

2. The effects of this realization may be important for young adults as well as older ones.

3. People of all ages will be able to relax and enjoy their lives when they realize that life gets better as we age.

4. Your own thesis statement: _____

_____

_____

Your Own Writing

Finding Out More

A. *You may want to learn more about the topic you chose. Plan and write three or four specific questions that you could ask people to find out more about your topic. Work with a partner and your teacher to refine your questions.*

_____

_____

_____

_____

_____

_____

B. *Interview several people. Ask your questions, ask follow-up questions, and take notes. Use quotation marks if you record someone's exact words. Add new information to the cause-effect web on page 129. Be sure to note the sources for your information.*

C. *Look at your interview notes.*

- Write two or three sentences about what each person said about the causes and/or effects related to your topic.

- Combine what you have learned from your interviews with your own ideas on page 129.

- You may want to use a T-chart to organize your ideas into major points and minor points.

D. Checking in. *Share your information with a partner. Did your partner . . .*

- ask at least three questions in each interview?

- make connections between causes and effects of happiness or stress?

- use quotation marks to indicate someone's exact words?

- use at least three reliable sources?

Use this information when you write your essay.

Planning Your Introduction

A. *First, decide if you are writing a cause essay or an effect essay.*

_____ I am writing about the causes of _____

_____ I am writing about the effects of _____

B. *List the background information you will need to include in your introduction. What is the specific situation you will be writing about? What are its causes or effects?*

_____

_____

_____

_____

C. *Write a draft of your thesis statement. Make sure your thesis statement clearly states whether you will focus on causes or effects of the situation. Look back at your freewriting, webs, and notes to help you.*

_____

_____

D. **Checking in.** *Share your plans for your introductory paragraph with a partner. Did your partner . . .*

- provide a context and describe the situation clearly?

- summarize either the causes or effects of the situation?

- write a thesis statement that clearly focuses on either causes or effects?

E. *Tell your partner what you like about his or her thesis statement. If you have any suggestions for improving it, share them. Then tell your partner what kind of supporting evidence you expect to see in his or her essay, based on the thesis statement.*

F. *Based on your partner's feedback, you may want to rewrite your thesis statement.*

■ THE BODY

The body of a cause-effect essay will develop and support your response to the assignment you chose. Remember that the body paragraphs will focus on either the causes or effects, but not both.

You will need at least two body paragraphs in your cause-effect essay.

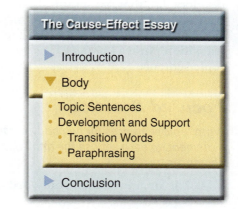

The Cause-Effect Essay

► Introduction

▼ Body
- Topic Sentences
- Development and Support
  - Transition Words
  - Paraphrasing

► Conclusion

Focus on Causes
Introduction
Background information on effects
Thesis statement on causes
Body Paragraph 1: Cause 1
Body Paragraph 2: Cause 2
Body Paragraph 3: Cause 3 (Optional)
Conclusion

Focus on Effects
Introduction
Background information on causes
Thesis statement on effects
Body Paragraph 1: Effect 1
Body Paragraph 2: Effect 2
Body Paragraph 3: Effect 3 (Optional)
Conclusion

Writing Topic Sentences

As with other types of essays, the body paragraphs in a cause-effect essay will build on the controlling idea expressed in the thesis statement. Each body paragraph begins with a topic sentence that states the main idea of that paragraph. If the focus of your cause-effect essay is *causes*, each topic sentence will state a cause or a reason something has happened. Likewise, if your essay focuses on *effects*, each topic sentence will state an effect or result of something that has happened.

As you learned in previous units, the topic sentence may also have certain types of transition words such as *the first*, *another*, *in addition to*, or *not only . . . but also* that help connect the main ideas of the body paragraphs.

Examples:

Cause Essay

Thesis Statement: There are two main reasons that I think people are happier when they are older.

Topic Sentence 1: The first reason is that they have less stress in daily life.

Topic Sentence 2: Another likely reason is that they have more free time to enjoy things that they want to rather than have to do.

Effect Essay

Thesis Statement: There are two important effects of people becoming happier as they get older.

Topic Sentence 1: First an increase in happiness helps aging people be more relaxed on a daily basis.

Topic Sentence 2: Just as people might become more relaxed, they might also stop worrying about growing old.

Notice that each of these examples states either the cause or the effect that will be developed in that paragraph. In the examples for a cause essay, the writer uses ordinal transitions, such as *first* and *another*, to connect the ideas between paragraphs. In the examples for an effect essay, the writer begins the second topic sentence with the transition phrase *(just) as . . . also* and then restates the controlling idea of the previous topic sentence.

Focused Practice

Write topic sentences for two body paragraphs that build on the controlling idea of each thesis statement. In each set use the transition words and phrases indicated to connect the two topic sentences.

A. Use ordinal transition words.

1. **Thesis Statement:** I think that there are two important reasons why people become happier as they age.
   (they do not have the pressures of work / they have fewer family responsibilities)

   Topic Sentence 1: *The first reason* _____

   Topic Sentence 2: *Another reason* _____

2. **Thesis Statement:** I believe that there are two significant effects of people becoming happier as they age.
   (they are more open to new experiences / the quality of their relationships improves)

   Topic Sentence 1: _____

   Topic Sentence 2: _____

B. Use a transition word or phrase such as *(just) as . . . also*, or *in addition to*, or *not only . . . but also* and restate the main idea from the first topic sentence.

1. **Thesis Statement:** I think that there are two important reasons why people become happier as they age.
   (they have more life experience / they have increased self-confidence)

   Topic Sentence 1: _____

   Topic Sentence 2: _____

2. **Thesis Statement:** I believe that there are two significant effects of people becoming happier as they age.
   (they connect more easily with others / they appreciate the "little things" in life)

   Topic Sentence 1: _____

   Topic Sentence 2: _____

Developing a Body Paragraph

Body paragraphs develop and support the controlling idea in your topic sentences. As you develop your ideas, it is important to support your thesis about the cause-effect relationship with as much evidence as possible. You can support your ideas with examples, facts, or statements from experts or relevant anecdotes. Your support needs to come from reliable sources such as reputable newspapers, journals, or experts in the field.

An effective way to report supporting details is by *paraphrasing*. When you paraphrase, you put someone else's ideas into your own words. A paraphrase includes only the original ideas, not your personal thoughts or opinions on the topic.

Paraphrasing can be challenging. Sometimes it will take you several tries to get your writing to match the original idea without copying it word for word. Look at this example.

Example:

Original: "These results say there are distinctive patterns here," [Professor Stone] said, "and it's worth some research efforts to try to figure out what's going on. Why at age 50 does something seem to start to change?" (Paragraph 10)

Paraphrase: Professor Stone believes that more studies should be done to determine why people seem to become happier after they turn 50 years old.

In academic writing it is essential that you credit the source of the ideas, that is, the person or text you are taking the ideas from. A common way to refer to a source is with *according to.*

source   information
According to a recent Gallup poll, people seem to get happier as they get older.

You can also use several other expressions to name your source and include any relevant identifying information.

Examples:

In [name]'s opinion, . . .

In Professor Oswald's opinion, the findings of the Gallup poll are significant and encouraging.

A [source] shows that . . .

A recent Gallup poll **shows that** people seem to become happier as they get older.

[Name], [title and affiliation] believes that . . .

Dr. Stone, a psychology professor at the State University of New York at Stony Brook, believes that these findings raise other questions that should be studied in the future.

It is [title] [name]'s belief that . . .

It is Professor Oswald's belief that the findings of the Gallup poll are significant and encouraging.

Focused Practice

A. *Review paragraph 8 on page 124. Then complete each paraphrase with the words from the box. Use each word only once.*

anger	happiness	stress
enjoyment	sadness	worry

1. _____*Sadness*_____ reaches its height when a person is 50 years old. Then it

declines for the next 20 years. It rises again in the mid-80s.

2. _____ begins to decrease after the teenage years are over.

3. _____ doesn't change much until people are 50. After that, it declines

dramatically.

4. _____ decreases until the age of 50, and then it rises until we are 75.

After that, it goes down slightly but it never goes down to the point it was at 50. The

same holds true for _____.

5. _____ begins to go down starting at 22 years old. It is at its lowest

level by the time people reach their mid-80s.

B. *Write sentences that include the information and the source. Use **According to** and other appropriate expressions. Follow the example.*

1. **Information:** Demark is the happiest country in the world, followed by Malta, Switzerland, Iceland, Ireland, and Canada.

   Source: Researchers at the World Database of Happiness at Erasmus University, Holland

   According to researchers at the World Database of Happiness at Erasmus

   University in Holland, Demark is the happiest country in the world, followed by

   Malta, Switzerland, Iceland, Ireland, and Canada.

2. **Information:** Children who were hugged more often grew up to be happier adults.

   Source: A study conducted at Harvard University

   _____

   _____

   _____

3. Information: It feels better to come in third place when you are not expecting it than it does when you come in second.

     Source: Graham Winters, Australian Olympic Teams psychologist

_____

_____

_____

4. Information: Among the things that made people happy were sports, music, and dancing.

     Source: Pioneering social psychologist Professor Michael Argyle, who studied happiness

_____

_____

_____

5. Information: Laughing lowers stress hormones and strengthens the immune system.

     Source: Gene Wallenstein, author of the book _Mind, Stress, and Emotion: The New Science of Mood_

_____

_____

_____

6. Information: The number one reason for stress is money. The countries most stressed about money are Malaysia, China, Singapore, and the United States.

     Source: A 2009 CNN poll

_____

_____

_____

7. Information: Dark chocolate reduces stress hormones.

     Source: Research conducted at the Nestle Research Center in Lausanne, Switzerland and published in the _Journal of Proteome Research_

_____

_____

_____

C. *Look at paragraph 11 on page 125. Then use the information to paraphrase Dr. Stone's idea from the following quotation. Be sure to credit your source.*

Quotation: "These are four reasonable candidates," Dr. Stone said, "but they don't make much difference."

Paraphrase: _____

_____

D. *Review your notes from your interviews and your research. Complete the chart.*

- Write supporting details or quotations from your interviews and research in the Information column.
- Write where you got the information or quotation in the Source column.
- Note why this information is important in the third column.

Information from the Text or Quotation	Source	Why This Information Is Important in Your Essay
1.		
2.		
3.		

E. *Write sentences that paraphrase the information from the chart above and give credit to the source. You may want to use some of these sentences in your essay.*

1. _____

_____

2. _____

_____

3. _____

_____

Your Own Writing

Planning Your Body Paragraphs

A. *Before you begin writing your body paragraphs, complete the following outline. Copy your thesis statement from page 134.*

- Write a topic sentence for each of the body paragraphs.

- Provide supporting details for each of the body paragraphs.

Cause-Effect Essay

▶ Thesis Statement: _____

_____

▶ Body Paragraph 1

    ▶ Topic Sentence 1: _____

    _____

        ▶ Supporting Details:

          • _____

          • _____

          • _____

          • _____

▶ Body Paragraph 2

    ▶ Topic Sentence 2: _____

    _____

        ▶ Supporting Details:

          • _____

          • _____

          • _____

          • _____

▶ Body Paragraph 3 (Optional)

   ▶ Topic Sentence 3: _____

   _____

      ▶ Supporting Details:

         • _____

         • _____

         • _____

         • _____

B. **Checking in.** *Share your outline with a partner. Did your partner . . .*

   • clearly state a cause or an effect in each topic sentence?

   • provide interesting and relevant supporting details?

   • present the causes or effects in an order that makes sense?

C. *Based on your partner's feedback, you may want to rewrite parts of your outline.*

■ THE CONCLUSION

As with other types of essays you have written, the conclusion is where you wrap up or close your essay. First, return to the general idea from your thesis statement. Some writers also use a transitional expression such as *In conclusion* or *In summary* to indicate that this is the concluding paragraph. Then, they end with a concluding strategy. In a cause-effect essay you might choose one of the following strategies:

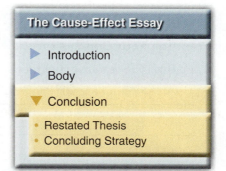

The Cause-Effect Essay

▶ Introduction
▶ Body
▼ Conclusion
   • Restated Thesis
   • Concluding Strategy

1. Propose a solution for the negative causes or effects you have described.

   • What should people do to identify and/or eliminate the causes of unhappiness or stress in their lives?

   • What should people do to reduce or eliminate the negative effects of unhappiness or stress?

2. Comment on the significance of your analysis.

   • Why might your view be important or interesting to the reader or society?

Focused Practice

Read the following essay assignment and the model of a concluding paragraph and then answer the questions with a partner.

What do you think causes people to become happier as they get older?

> There are many possible factors that might cause older people to feel happier. As Dr. Stone suggests in the *New York Times* article, more research is needed if we are going to identify specific reasons for this trend. However, I don't think we need to identify the exact reasons. We simply need to spread the word: getting older is not a bad thing. I am certain that many people would look at getting older in a more positive way if they were aware of these Gallup poll results. When I am eighty, I hope that I will be as happy as this report suggests I will be.

1. Underline the sentence(s) that restates the thesis statement.
2. Circle the phrase(s) that the writer uses to credit the source(s) of information he used.
3. What concluding strategy did the writer use?

Your Own Writing

Planning Your Conclusion

A. *How will you rephrase your thesis statement in the conclusion? List your ideas here.*

_____

_____

B. *What strategy will you use to close the essay?*

_____

_____

C. Checking in. *Share your ideas with a partner. Did your partner . . .*

- rephrase the thesis statement in a new and interesting way?

- choose an effective concluding strategy?

Writing Your First Draft

A. *Review your notes on pages 129, 134, and 141–142. Then write the first draft of your paragraph. When you are finished, give your paragraph a working title. Hand in your draft to your teacher.*

> **Tip for Writers**
>
> When you write your first draft, remember that **you need reliable sources.** Always say where your supporting details come from. When you quote or paraphrase a person's ideas, always give the person's name and where that person is from to indicate that this person is a reliable source.

Revising your work is an essential part of the writing process. This is your opportunity to be sure that your essay has all the important pieces and that it is clear.

Focused Practice

A. *You have read parts of this cause-effect essay already. Now read the entire essay to see how the parts fit together.*

Getting Better with Age

In our culture we seem to value being young—or at least keeping our bodies looking that way. The assumption is that "youth equals happiness" and "aging equals unhappiness." We ignore evidence that suggests that the opposite is true: aging can bring happiness. No one seems to notice the radiant, satisfied smile of a grandmother enjoying her favorite activities, such as playing with her grandchildren or working in her garden. Who really pays attention to a group of worry-free gray-haired old men sitting together, trading stories or playing cards? People automatically think that being younger means being happier. However, the results of a recent Gallup poll described in the *New York Times* clearly contradict this view. The reality, according to the poll, is that people seem to get happier as they get older. The poll did not explain why; however, I think there are three likely reasons that people gradually get happier as they age.

One reason that older people might be happier is that they no longer have to worry about work or their careers. Most middle-aged people have to juggle home life and work life. Whether you are a farmer, a grocer, or a banker, work is demanding. It often feels like there is not enough time in the day to do everything that needs to be done. This may leave people feeling discouraged or overwhelmed. Not only do they have to do their jobs well, but they also have to think about salary and advancement. In almost any work environment there is at least some competition to stay on top. Even for people who like their jobs, this competition can cause negative emotions, such as insecurity or doubt in one's abilities or one's future. Steven Hsu, a retired corporate executive, reported that he was extremely surprised by how much better he felt after he stopped working. "Looking back I can see how tense I was—trying to do my job well and trying to work my way up the corporate ladder," Hsu said. He added that he would make some changes if

(continued)

he could do it again. People who no longer have to work do not have to face work pressures or "office politics" any more.

In addition to less stress at work, older people have less stress at home. Middle-aged people have to worry about their responsibilities at home. While home may be a welcome change from work, there is still a lot to do there. Bills have to be paid, and the place has to be cleaned. People with a spouse or a partner need to work hard to maintain a healthy relationship. Those with children have the added responsibility of feeding, clothing, and educating their kids—and these are just the basics. There is no denying that one's home life can be a source of great joy. However, sometimes it can feel like too much. This directly affects our feelings about life. We might feel depressed by it all. All of these factors can weigh us down so that our attitude is not one of peace and enjoyment but just the opposite. John and Barbara Serafina are raising three daughters, the last of whom will be going off to college in six years. They noted that they were looking forward to the last one being out of the house. They love their daughters and enjoyed raising them, but they can also see a little relief coming without the daily pressures of parenthood. Clearly the Serafinas are not alone in this.

A final possible explanation why people become happier as they age is that their attitude toward themselves changes. It could be a chemical change in the brain. However, on some level, people may become more content with who they are as individuals and where they are in life. We don't have to prove ourselves to anyone. We know who we are. My father, a very successful accountant, worked hard all his life. Every day he had to keep his clients happy by doing a good job and building their confidence in him. He also had to find new clients. There was a lot more to his job than just crunching numbers. I'm sure that there were times he doubted that he was doing a good enough job as an accountant and as a father. Today, he feels different. He told me in an interview for this essay that he looks back and knows that he did his best as an accountant and as a parent. He knows that he wasn't perfect, but he recognizes that he tried, and now he can relax and enjoy the results of his hard work. Like my father, other senior citizens may have a more relaxed, more patient, view of themselves. This may make the later years of life more pleasant.

(continued)

There are many possible factors that might cause older people to feel happier. Dr. Arthur A. Stone stated in the *New York Times* article that more research is needed if we are going to identify the specific reasons for this trend. However, regardless of the reasons, it is important that we realize that life for most people does get better. Perhaps if more people recognize this fact, they will stop worrying about the passing of their youth and become confident that life does get better. When people do this, they may find that happiness may come much sooner than expected.

B. *Work with a partner. Answer the questions about the essay.*

1. What is the thesis statement? Underline it.

2. What are the writer's topic sentences? Underline them.

3. Are the body paragraphs about causes or effects? Write *cause* or *effect* beside each body paragraph.

4. What transition words or expressions connect the parts of the essay? Circle them.

5. What kinds of supporting details does the writer use in the body paragraphs? Label them *examples, facts, statements from experts* or *anecdotes*.

6. How does the writer acknowledge sources of the supporting details? Double underline two examples.

7. Which paragraph presents the most convincing cause? Put a check (✓) next to it and explain your choice to your partner.

8. What concluding strategy does the writer use? Label it as one of the two strategies on page 143.

C. Checking in. *Discuss your marked-up essay with another pair of students. Then in your group, share one thing about the essay that you found the most interesting. Explain your answer.*

Building Word Knowledge

Using Reporting Verbs. Use reporting verbs in your writing when you include quotations or paraphrase what someone else has said or written. As you know, the most common reporting word is *say* or *said*. Here are some other reporting verbs. They are also most commonly used in the past.

- stated (similar to *said* but more formal)
- claimed (an opinion without evidence)
- told (when the listener is mentioned)
- reported (factual information)
- added (an additional idea)
- noted (a small piece of information or brief comment)

A. *Find five reporting verbs in the sample essay on page 145. Circle them and notice how they are used. Then underline the other verbs in the same sentences. Notice the verb forms that the writer uses. Are they present or past?*

B. *Complete the sentences with a reporting verb from Building Word Knowledge above. Then compare your answers with a partner and explain your choices.*

1. The research team _____ that the results of their research were not conclusive and that they would continue to study the problem.

2. My uncle once _____ me that people are only as old as they feel inside.

3. The professor _____ that the exam would include an essay about aging, and he _____ that the students would not be able to use dictionaries in the exam.

4. My parents _____ that, when they retired, they wanted to move away from their small hometown and live in a large city.

5. Opponents of the solution _____ that there was little evidence to indicate that it would be effective.

6. The *New York Times* _____ that the Gallup poll surveyed more than 340,000 people across the United States.

Your Own Writing

Revising Your Draft

A. *Reread the first draft of your essay. Use the Revision Checklist to identify parts of your writing that might need improvement.*

B. *Review your plans and notes and your responses to the Revision Checklist. Then revise your first draft. Save your revised essay. You will look at it again in the next section.*

Revision Checklist

Did you . . .

☐ give enough background in your introduction?

☐ include a clear thesis statement?

☐ use topic sentences with transitions in your body paragraphs?

☐ develop the body paragraphs with supporting details such as examples, facts, quotations, or anecdotes?

☐ restate the controlling idea of the essay in your conclusion?

☐ use an effective concluding strategy?

☐ use reporting verbs correctly?

☐ use appropriate phrases to credit sources?

☐ paraphrase correctly?

☐ give your essay an interesting title?

■ GRAMMAR PRESENTATION

Before you hand in your revised essay, you must check it for any errors in grammar, punctuation, and spelling. In this section you will learn about direct and indirect reported speech. You will focus on this grammar when you edit and proofread your essay.

Direct and Indirect Speech

Grammar Notes	Examples
1. Direct speech (also called *quoted speech*) states the <u>exact words</u> that the speaker or writer used. In **writing**, put **quotation marks** before and after the words you are quoting. That speech (called the **quotation**) can go at the **beginning** or at the **end** of a sentence. Use a **comma** to separate the quotation from the rest of the sentence.	• Jane said**,** **"**I feel great. 60 is the new 40.**"** • **"**I feel great. 60 is the new 40**,"** Jane said.
2. Indirect speech (also called *reported speech*) reports what a speaker said <u>without using the exact words</u>. The word **that** can introduce indirect speech. **BE CAREFUL!** Do **NOT** use **quotation marks** with indirect speech	• Jane said that she felt great and that 60 was the new 40. • She said **that she felt great.** NOT: She said ~~"that she felt great."~~
3. Reporting verbs (such as **say** and **tell**) are usually in the **simple past** for both direct and indirect speech. Use **say** when you **do not mention the listener**. Use **tell** when you **mention the listener**. **BE CAREFUL!** Do **NOT use** **tell** when you don't mention the listener.	**DIRECT SPEECH:** • "I have been very stressed out lately," Andrei **said**. • "I have been very stressed out lately," Andrei **told** me. **INDIRECT SPEECH:** • Andrei **said that** he has been very stressed out lately. • Andrei **told me that** he has been very stressed out lately. NOT: Andrei ~~said me~~ that he has been very stressed out lately.

4. When the **reporting verb** is in the **simple past** (*said*, *told*), we often **change the verb tense** in the indirect speech statement.

The **simple present** in direct speech becomes the **simple past** in indirect speech.

- "I **don't want** a big birthday party," he said.
- He said that he **didn't want** a big birthday party.

The **simple past** in direct speech becomes **past perfect** in indirect speech.

- "I **enjoyed** every minute of my childhood," she said.
- She said that she **had enjoyed** every minute of her childhood.

5. You do **NOT have to change the tense** when you report:
a. something that was **just said**.

A: "I want to have lunch soon."
B: "Excuse me?"
A: I **said I want to have lunch soon**.
OR
   I **said I wanted to have lunch soon**.

b. something that is **still true**.

- I **said** that Gloria **is** 80 years old.
OR
- I **said** that Gloria **was** 80 years old.

c. a **general truth** or **scientific law**.

- The article said that people get happier as they get older, and researchers are not sure why.

DIRECT SPEECH:
- "It **could be** psychological changes," said Dr. Stone.

INDIRECT SPEECH:
- Dr. Stone said that it **could be** psychological changes.

USAGE NOTE: *Could* does not change in reported speech.

6. When the **reporting verb** is in the **simple present**, **do NOT change the verb tense** in the indirect speech statement.

USAGE NOTE: In newspapers, magazines, and on the TV and radio news, **reporting verbs** are often in the **simple present**.

- "It is something very deep and quite human," says the psychologist.
- The psychologist **says** that it **is** something very deep and quite human.
  NOT: The psychologist says that it ~~was~~ something very deep and quite human.
- Oswald **says** that it **is** something very deep and quite human."
  BUT:
- Oswald **said** that it **was** something very deep and quite human.

7. In **indirect speech**, make changes in **pronouns and possessives** to keep the speakers <u>original meaning</u>.

- Patrick told Dick, "I feel better about **my** life."

- Patrick told Dick that **he** felt better about **his** life.

Focused Practice

A. *Read these sentences in direct speech and write them in indirect speech. Use a reporting verb and add necessary punctuation. Change verb forms and pronouns as needed.*

1. "The secret of genius is to carry the spirit of the child into old age. . . ."
   —Aldous Huxley

   _____

   _____

2. "I could not, at any age, be content to take my place in a corner by the fireside and simply look on." —Eleanor Roosevelt

   _____

   _____

3. "Common sense is the collection of prejudices acquired by age eighteen."
   —Albert Einstein

   _____

   _____

B. *Read and edit a student's report about an interview. There are ten errors in the use of direct and indirect speech. The first error has already been corrected. Find and correct nine more.*

> Last week our group interviewed 20 people about the causes of stress in their lives. Here are two examples of causes of stress.
>
> One person reported that her life last year was especially stressful. She said
>
> that ~~my~~ *her* greatest source of stress is school. This woman was a college chemistry major. She said me that she never had enough time to complete her assignments. "I wanted to do all the required work, but there just aren't enough hours in the day," she told the interviewer. She added that she thinks her professors assigned unrealistic amounts of reading.
>
> A second person was an English professor, Dr. Rosalie Torres. Professor Torres says that even though she enjoyed her job, she still felt a lot of stress. On the day of the interview, she explained that she is very busy preparing for class, writing comments on her students' essays, and getting ready for two committee meetings.
>
> *(continued)*

She said it was always like that. "This took a lot of time," she added. However, she told that her biggest source of stress was actually childcare. With her busy work schedule, she tries to balance her busy work life and her family life. She said that she will spend as much time as possible with her family.

C. *Choose two interesting or important quotations from your interviews. Write the direct speech and then write the indirect speech. Use reporting verbs. These may be sentences you already have in your essay.*

1. Direct: _____

_____

Indirect: _____

_____

2. Direct: _____

_____

Indirect: _____

_____

Your Own Writing

Editing Your Draft

A. *Use the Editing Checklist to edit and proofread your essay.*

B. *Prepare a clean copy of the final draft of your essay and hand it in to your teacher.*

Editing Checklist

Did you . . .

☐ use direct and indirect speech correctly?

☐ use *say*, *tell*, and other reporting verbs correctly?

☐ use quotation marks before and after direct speech?

☐ use a comma to separate direct speech from the rest of the sentence?

☐ use the correct verb forms and pronouns in indirect speech?

☐ use correct verb forms, punctuation, and spelling in other parts of your essay?

☐ use and give credit to reliable sources?

UNIT 6

What to Do?

IN THIS UNIT   You will be writing an essay about a difficult decision. For this assignment you will decide how to organize your writing.

An ethical dilemma is a difficult situation in which you must choose between two or more alternatives. None of the alternatives is clearly right or wrong. For example, imagine that you work for a company and make a good salary. You love the work and the people. However, the company manufactures a product that is bad for the environment. Should you quit your job? Think of an ethical dilemma that you may have faced. What did you do?

Planning for Writing

■ BRAINSTORM

A. *Read about this dilemma.*

> ### The Race to the Top
>
> Scientists have discovered a new planet they've named Planet X. It has many natural resources that countries on Earth could benefit from. The location of this planet is also very strategic. A country with weapons on this planet could point them at Earth and potentially control or harm the world. Country A and Country B both super powers with a history of animosity for each other, are considering traveling to Planet X to claim it. They have the technology, but the cost of space exploration is extremely high. However, the country that reaches Planet X first will control it.
>
> The citizens of Country A are not interested in space exploration. They have consistently voted against funding. Domestic problems, including unemployment, health care, and education, are more pressing. Yet, some leaders of Country A believe that ignoring Country B's interest could have serious consequences. Citizens of Country B may have concerns similar to those of Country A.
>
> You are a member of an important group of government officials in Country A. The president of your country is expecting your group to analyze the situation and make a recommendation about what your country should do regarding Planet X.

B. Using Graphic Organizers. In previous units you have learned to use different graphic organizers such as T-charts, problem-solution charts, and cause-effect webs to help you plan your essays. However, when you plan and write an academic essay, you may want to use a variety of graphic organizers to help you think about the topic from different perspectives.

Read "The Race to the Top" above. Divide into three groups. Each group will use one graphic organizer to analyze the issue. Each group will make a recommendation to the president of Country A and share the recommendation with the class.

Group 1: Use a T-chart (see page 8) to analyze the advantages and disadvantages of Country A pursuing Planet X. Write "Advantages" on one side and "Disadvantages" on the other.

Group 2: Use a problem-solution chart (see page 63) to analyze the problem and the possible solutions. Write the problem in the upper left box. Then fill in the other boxes.

Group 3: Use a cause-effect web (see page 129) to analyze what might cause Country A to pursue Planet X and what the effects might be. Write "Pursuing Planet X" in the center oval.

C. *Present the ideas from your graphic organizer to the class. Take notes as you listen to each of the other groups. Discuss the following questions with a partner.*

1. What were the advantages and disadvantages that Group 1 presented?

2. What problem did Group 2 identify and what solution(s) did they propose?

3. What causes and effects did Group 3 identify and discuss?

4. What recommendation did each group make to the president?

Read the lecture notes and assignment posted on a professor's course web page.

Ethics 101

Professor N. Nakamaru

Assignment #6: Read these lecture notes and prepare for a class discussion.
Due: Thursday, January 29

THE PRISONER'S DILEMMA

1 The prisoner's dilemma is a classic case study, or game, used in the social sciences, to look at and understand cooperation and competition in political, business, and social situations that involve making ethical decisions or choices. Here is the typical scenario:[1]

2 The police suspect two men of robbing a bank. The police arrest the two suspects and put them in separate jail cells to question them. They need more evidence in order to convict[2] one or both of them.

3 The police captain tells each man that he has two choices:

4 "You can confess or remain silent. If you confess, you will go free, and we will use the evidence that you give us to send your buddy[3] to prison for ten years. If you *both* confess, then you will each go to prison for 5 years. If you both stay silent, then you'll each spend 6 months in prison because, when you were arrested, you were carrying unlicensed guns. Now, I'm going to give you some time to think. Sleep on it, and give me your answer in the morning. Oh, and by the way, you won't know what your buddy says until after this investigation is over."

5 **What should the prisoners do: confess or keep silent?**

6 In the game, the players, or prisoners, want to get the maximum payoff, the best result, while reducing negative results for themselves. Players have the option to "defect" or "cooperate." *Defecting* is betraying other players by giving evidence to convict them and to pursue personal self-interest. *Cooperating* is choosing the option that is beneficial to the group. In the prisoner's dilemma, when prisoners give evidence against each other, they are defecting, and when they remain silent, they are cooperating.

7 Clearly for both prisoners there is a lot at stake—freedom or time in jail. If the players think carefully, they see that they can reduce (but not eliminate) their overall risk by cooperating. However, the problem is that players do not know how the other will choose.

8 Research shows that a player is more likely to defect in order to avoid greater negative consequences for himself. However, while defecting is the most common choice, it is also the choice that typically produces the worst outcome for the individual and the group.

9 Interestingly, researchers have also found that if the game is played repeatedly, players eventually begin to cooperate more because of the threat of increased punishment. Once a player becomes aware of the choices that another player makes, his reputation may suffer and others will not trust him. Choosing based on self-interest may make things increasingly worse for him.

---

[1] **scenario:** a situation that could possibly happen but has not happened yet
[2] **convict:** to prove or officially announce that someone is guilty of a crime after trial in a court of law
[3] **buddy:** (very informal) a male friend or associate

10 In daily life we may face similar ethical dilemmas. The decisions we make often have an impact on others, as well as on ourselves, and life is no game! If we are lucky, we find ourselves in a "win-win" situation, where the result is beneficial for everyone involved.

11 Unfortunately, our choices are usually complicated. Sometimes we have to decide how much risk we are willing to accept for ourselves and those around us. Benefiting yourself is not always wrong; however, the principles of ethics remind us to consider the cost to everyone involved.

12 Now read this scenario and be prepared to discuss the question that follows.

The Economics Paper

13   Sofia Simons is a college student majoring in nursing. She is taking an economics class that was recommended by her best friend, David. Many weeks into the semester, Sofia clearly sees that she is not a very strong student in this subject.

14   As the end of the semester approaches, Sofia has to write a 20-page final paper. Because she scored poorly on the midterm exam, she needs an "A" on this paper to pass the course. Sofia fears failing the course because this would result in her losing her scholarship, her only way of paying for school. There is a lot riding on this paper.

15   Last night she found an essay online that answers the question the professor assigned. The users of this website who rated this essay say that it is an "A" paper. She is aware that submitting writing that is not her own is plagiarism. She understands that students caught plagiarizing may be expelled from the college.

16   Furthermore, in this class the professor grades on a bell curve,[4] which means that only a certain number of "A's" will be given. Therefore, Sofia's "A" on her paper could mean that other students, like David, might get lower grades, meaning that they may risk losing their scholarships, or experience other negative results.

17 **In Sofia's situation, is using the online essay the best choice? When answering this question, you might do one of the following: consider advantages and disadvantages, focus on the effects of Sofia's choice on her life and her classmates' lives, or propose a possible solution or solutions to Sofia's problem.**

---

[4] **grade on a bell curve:** to use a method of giving grades (A, B, C, D, and F) designed to produce a pre-determined distribution of grades among students in a class. That is, the professor will give more "C" (average) grades and fewer A's (outstanding) and F's (failing).

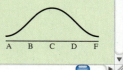

Building Word Knowledge

Using Idioms. To write well, it is important to use a variety of appropriate terms and expressions. An idiom is a group of words used together that have a different meaning from the ordinary meaning of the individual words. Here are some common idioms from the reading.

a win-win situation: a situation in which everyone benefits or profits in some way; there are no losers

be at stake: when something of great value might be lost if a plan of action is not successful

be/have a lot riding on: a situation in which success or a desired result depends on the positive results of a certain event (similar to *be at stake*)

sleep on it: to wait before making an important decision

Find these idioms in the reading on page 156. Notice how they are used.

Focused Practice

A. *Review the reading. In the prisoner's dilemma, how long will the prisoners be in jail? Who will go free? Complete the sentences in the chart. Then check your answers with a partner's.*

	Prisoner B Stays Silent (Cooperates)	**Prisoner B Confesses** (Defects, Betrays)
Prisoner A Stays Silent (Cooperates)	Prisoner A *will spend 6 months in jail.* Prisoner B	Prisoner A Prisoner B
Prisoner A Confesses (Defects, Betrays)	Prisoner A Prisoner B	Prisoner A Prisoner B

B. *Write a short response for each question. Then discuss your answers in groups.*

1. According to the reading, what is the problem that each prisoner faces?

_____

_____

2. According to the reading, why do players choose to defect rather than cooperate?

_____

_____

3. According to the reading, which choice is typically more beneficial to all the players? Why is it the better choice?

_____

_____

4. After you read what the police captain told the prisoner, which choice did you think the prisoner should make? Why?

_____

_____

C. *Look at the assignment at the end of "The Economics Paper" on page 157. Freewrite for ten minutes in response to the professor's assignment. Then share your ideas with the class.*

D. *Read the* Tip for Writers. *Work with a partner. Discuss your writing from Exercise C. If you were writing an essay in response to the professor's assignment, what would the purpose of your essay be? Look back at the graphic organizers described on page 155. List some ways you could organize parts of your essay to accomplish your purpose.*

_____

_____

_____

_____

_____

_____

Tip for Writers

In Unit 1 you learned that the three basic purposes for writing are to persuade, to inform, or to entertain. In an academic essay, you may **choose to organize various parts of your essay in different ways to accomplish your purpose**. For example, in a persuasive essay, you may decide to write about the causes and effects of a situation in part of your essay to persuade your reader to agree with your point of view.

Writing an Essay Using Multiple Organizational Structures

You are going to write an essay about an ethical dilemma. In previous units, you have written essays with different types of organizational structures: persuasive, problem-solution, compare-contrast, and cause-effect. When you write an essay in a college course, however, you may incorporate more than one organizational structure. For example, within a persuasive or problem-solution essay, you may decide to explain the causes and effects of a situation or compare and contrast two issues. For the assignment in this unit, your basic purpose will be to persuade your readers to agree with your opinion about an ethical dilemma. You will use a different organizational structure in each body paragraph to support your opinion.

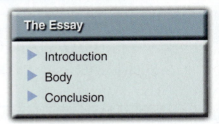

The Essay

► Introduction
► Body
► Conclusion

Remember that all essays contain three parts.

Step 1   Prewriting

For an essay that uses different organizational structures, the prewriting step involves deciding which of these structures will most effectively support your thesis. For example, in an essay about what choice someone should make in a difficult situation, it may be important to explain the causes of the situation and the effects of the choices, or propose specific solutions that would support a particular choice. The prewriting step also includes thinking of information that will best support your ideas.

Your Own Writing

Choosing Your Assignment

A. *Choose Assignment 1 or Assignment 2.*

1. It is often difficult to know when to put your own interests ahead of someone else's, especially when that person is a family member. Read *Family Matters* below. In your opinion, what is the best choice for Helen or Tim? To support your point of view, you may want to discuss the advantages and disadvantages, or the causes and/or effects, of certain choices. You may also want to present solution(s) to the problem.

Family Matters

Tim and Helen Rhee are brother and sister. Tim has been unemployed for a year. Helen is employed, but she is miserable in her current job. She feels stuck because she has no chance for future promotion and is actively seeking better opportunities for her future.

Tim's best friend, Mike Abdullah, tells him about a job opening in his company. Mike is a manager in the company and could get Tim an interview. Tim decides to apply for the job.

As Helen listens to Tim's animated description of the job, she becomes quite interested. She thinks that she would like to apply for the job. She knows that she is qualified for it, and having this job would give her hope for the future. However, she also realizes how excited her brother is about the prospect of getting the job.

➡

For Tim, having this job would give him the financial security he has wanted for the past year. It would also restore the confidence he's lost after being unemployed for so long. However, he suspects that he might not be qualified for the job. He knows how his sister feels about her present work situation and that she has the qualifications the company is looking for.

2. It is often difficult to know when to put your own interests ahead of someone else's, especially when that person is a family member. Read *Time Management* below. In your opinion, what is the best choice for Joe? To support your point of view, you may want to discuss the advantages and disadvantages, or the causes and/or effects, of certain choices. You may also want to present solution(s) to the problem.

Time Management

After graduating from college with a bachelor's degree in mathematics, Joe McCarthy landed a good job, got married, and within a few years, had two children.

Joe is committed to his family. He and his wife Debbie believe in maintaining a close connection with each other and the children. As the children approach their teens, Joe and Debbie are concerned about giving both of them sufficient guidance and attention. They agree that their children need the support, influence, and presence of both parents during these formative years.

Joe also loves his work and is very successful. His company admires his dedication, and his annual reviews are always very positive. Joe is eager to advance in his company, and would welcome the extra responsibility. An increased salary would mean a better standard of living for the family and would also make college for the children easier to manage. To get the promotion he wants and deserves, Joe realizes that he will need to get a Master's degree. A local university has an evening-and-weekend program that would allow him to continue working full-time. However, working full-time and going to school will take up most of his free time for at least the next two years. He would not be able to spend much time with his family.

B. *Freewrite for ten minutes on your assignment. Here are some questions to get you started:*

- What do you think is the best choice for the person with this dilemma? Why?

- Have you, or someone you know, ever been faced with a similar dilemma? How did you decide what to do? What was the result of your choice?

C. *On separate pieces of paper, complete all three graphic organizers about the assignment you chose. Fill in as much information as you can. You will have a chance to review, change, or add information later in the unit.*

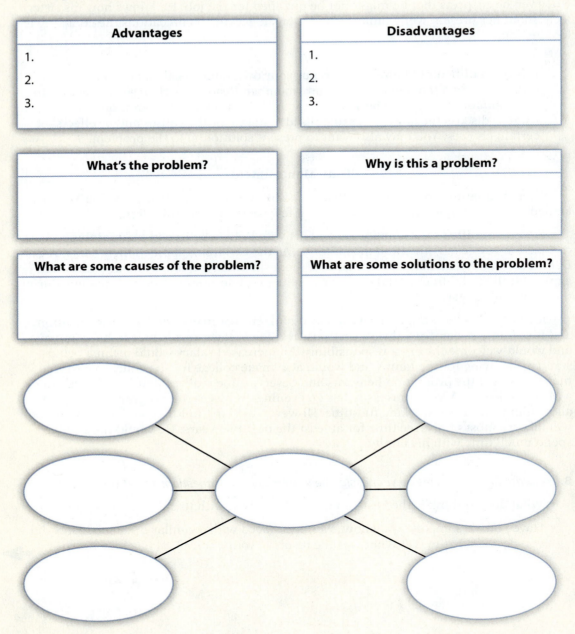

Advantages	Disadvantages
1.	1.
2.	2.
3.	3.

What's the problem?	Why is this a problem?

What are some causes of the problem?	What are some solutions to the problem?

D. Checking in. *Work with a partner who chose the same assignment. Discuss the information you wrote in your graphic organizers in Exercise C. Did your partner . . .*

- clearly state an opinion about the best choice for the person with the dilemma?

- explain his or her opinion?

- complete each graphic organizer with relevant information?

Share your opinion about your partner's topic. Based on your discussion, make changes and additions to your writing and graphic organizers.

■ THE INTRODUCTION

As you have studied in previous units, an introductory paragraph has two main parts. *Background information* helps the reader understand the topic and the **thesis statement** presents the controlling idea of the essay. As in other essays, the thesis may be one or two sentences.

In this essay, your basic purpose is to convince your reader to share your point of view. Therefore, your *thesis statement* should express the controlling idea of the essay—your opinion about the question in the assignment. It should also include persuasive language: words and phrases that suggest that you are giving an opinion. You learned some of these words and phrases in Units 1 and 2.

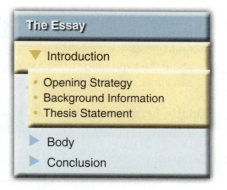

The background information should also stimulate your reader's interest in the topic. There is a variety of ways to begin your essay that will encourage your reader to continue reading. We call these *opening strategies.* Here are some common types of opening strategies:

1. Ask a provocative question.

2. Begin a story that will be finished in the concluding paragraph.

3. Begin with a relevant quotation or statistic.

Look at this introductory paragraph in an essay about Planet X.

Example:

>   Instead of spending billions of dollars on a space project, our government needs to create job opportunities so that people can afford to live. Furthermore, there are other problems that cannot be ignored: the sorry state of our healthcare and education systems. Given these concerns, why would this country consider investing in a new multi-billion-dollar space project? Yes, exploring a new planet will be exciting for some, and it may even give this country safety or power over other countries. However, this proposal is not worth the investment.

Notice that the previous paragraph has no opening strategy. Now look at the same paragraph with an opening strategy.

Example:

>   <u>Would exploring a new planet give this country long-term safety or power over other countries</u>? It might. However, there are significant problems in this country that must be addressed first. Our government needs to create job opportunities so that people can afford to live. Furthermore, the state of our healthcare system is frightening and our educational system desperately needs improvement. Given these concerns, why would this country consider investing in a new multi-billion-dollar space project? I strongly feel that the proposal to explore Planet X is not worth the investment.

For the preceding example, the writer chose to open the paragraph with a provocative question. The writer also could have chosen a *relevant quotation* or *statistic*. Look at the same paragraph that opens with a statistic.

Example:

> As of last week, 15.9% of our citizens are unemployed, and 10% have been unable to find work for 26 weeks or more. Yet, some government leaders want us to invest in a multi-billion-dollar space project. There are significant problems in this country that need to be addressed before we even think about the exploration of Planet X. Our government needs to create job opportunities so that people can afford to live. Furthermore . . .

Finally, here is a example of the paragraph that opens with a *story*. The story might be continued through the essay and finished in the conclusion.

Example:

> Michael Green has always been a hard worker. However, in this economy, his company has had to lay off many of its employees. After a three-month search for a new job, Michael is still jobless. The rate of unemployment in his state clearly shows that Michael is not alone. Our government needs to create job opportunities so that people like Michael can afford to live. Furthermore . . .

Focused Practice

A. *Read the following essay assignment and check (✓) which information you might use as background for an introductory paragraph on this topic. Then identify items that use an opening strategy and write the number of that strategy from page 163 on the line. If there is no opening strategy, write N. Discuss your choices with a partner.*

Read "The Prisoner's Dilemma" and "The Economics Paper." In a case like Sofia's, do you think that using the online paper is the best choice? To support your point of view, you may want to consider the advantages and disadvantages of using the paper, the effects of her choice on Sofia and her classmates, and possible solutions to Sofia's problem.

1. _____ According to one expert, 53 percent of students admit to plagiarism, but many are unsure about whether or not it is cheating. _____

2. _____ David is Sofia's best friend. It was on his recommendation that she took an economics course in her third year of nursing school. _____

3. _____ During final exams last semester, my best friend was caught cheating and was expelled from school. Sofia Simons faces the possibility of the same thing happening to her and the consequences that go with it. _____

4. _____ Have you ever been in a situation that didn't seem to have a way out? Sofia Simons seems to be in this kind of situation. _____

5. _____ Sofia Simons is in danger of failing her economics class, but she found a paper online that could help her pass. She needs to pass in order to keep her scholarship. However, if she gets caught plagiarizing, the consequences could be very serious. _____

6. _____ Sofia Simons is a nursing major in her third year of college. She is planning to pursue a career in public health nursing. _____

B. *Review the essay assignment in Exercise A. Then write a thesis statement in one or two sentences using the information given.*

1. Topic: Using the online paper

   Opinion: It would be a terrible mistake.

   Persuasive Language: There is no doubt (that)

   _____

   _____

2. Topic: Using the online paper in order to pass her economics course

   Opinion: This would be completely irresponsible.

   Persuasive Language: In my opinion

   _____

   _____

3. Topic: Using the online paper to help her pass the economics course

   Opinion: For Sofia, this is the best decision.

   Persuasive Language: Clearly

   _____

   _____

4. Topic: Using the online paper

   Opinion: The risks outweigh the benefits. It would be foolish for Sofia to use it.

   Persuasive Language: I believe

   _____

   _____

5. Topic: Using the online paper

   Opinion: The benefits outweigh the risks.

   Persuasive Language: There is no denying (that)

   _____

   _____

C. *Look again at the essay assignment in Exercise A and the following introductory paragraph. Answer the questions. Then discuss your answers with a partner.*

> What would you risk for a passing grade in one of your courses? Sofia Simons is a college student struggling to pass her economics class. Because she did poorly on the midterm exam, she needs to get an "A" on her final paper in order to pass the course and keep the scholarship that allows her to pay for her classes. Interestingly, she may have a possible solution to her problem. Sofia came across an economics paper on a website that offers student papers for a fee. The paper she found was rated as excellent, and it covers the same topic that Sofia's professor assigned. At the moment, she is debating whether or not to use this paper. I believe that the risks outweigh the benefits in this situation. It would be foolish for Sofia to use the online paper.

1. Which sentences provide the background information? Underline them.
2. What opening strategy does the writer use? Do you think it is effective? Why?
3. What is the thesis statement? Double underline it.
4. What does the writer think Sofia should do? Why?
5. What persuasive language does the writer use in the thesis statement? Circle it.

Your Own Writing

Finding Out More

A. *You may want to learn more about the topic you chose for your essay.*

- Interview three to five people about the dilemma you chose.
- Read the assignment to your interviewees. Then ask them to react to the situation.
- Ask follow-up questions to find out more about their point of view.

B. *Take notes on what you found out. Write down what people told you. Highlight interesting ideas and supporting details that you might use in your essay. Organize your interview notes in a way that makes sense to you. Add to the graphic organizers you started on page 162.*

C. Checking in. *Share your information with a partner. Did your partner...*

- interview three to five people about this dilemma?
- gather enough facts and details about the interviewees' reactions to the dilemma?
- get a surprising point of view from anyone who was interviewed?

Use this information when you write your essay.

Planning Your Introduction

A. *What opening strategy will you use in your essay? Write it on the line.*

1. A provocative question: _____

2. A relevant quotation or statistic: _____

3. A brief, engaging story: _____

_____

B. *List the background information you will need to include in your introduction.*

_____

_____

C. *Write a draft of your thesis statement. Make sure your thesis statement responds to the question in the assignment, clearly expresses your opinion, and includes persuasive language. Look back at your freewriting and graphic organizers to help you.*

_____

_____

_____

D. Checking in. *Share your thesis statement with a partner. Did your partner...*

- respond to the question in the assignment?
- clearly express his or her opinion about the question?
- use persuasive language?

Tell your partner what you like about his or her thesis statement. If you have any suggestions for improving it, share them. Then tell your partner what kind of supporting evidence you expect to see in his or her essay, based on the thesis statement.

E. *Based on your partner's feedback, you may want to rewrite your thesis statement.*

■ THE BODY

When you wrote your essays in previous units, you organized each essay in a particular way. For example, you compared and contrasted two issues, or you identified a problem and alternative solutions. In this unit, you will use multiple organizational structures. Remember that the basic purpose of the essay will be to persuade your reader to agree with your point of view. The organizational structures you choose for your body paragraphs should be the most effective in supporting your thesis statement.

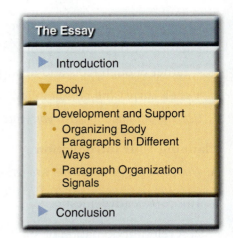

The Essay

▶ Introduction

▼ Body
   • Development and Support
   • Organizing Body Paragraphs in Different Ways
   • Paragraph Organization Signals

▶ Conclusion

Developing and Supporting Your Thesis Statement

As you have learned in previous units, the topic sentence in each body paragraph develops and supports the controlling idea in the thesis statement. The remaining sentences in each body paragraph develop and support the controlling idea of the topic sentence. Look at this example.

Example:

Thesis Statement: I believe that the risks outweigh the benefits in this situation. It would be foolish for Sofia to use the online paper.

Body Paragraph 1:

topic sentence

The main reason that I think it would be foolish for Sofia to use the paper is that, if she gets caught, she may not be able to continue her education at all. The college's plagiarism policy clearly states that she can be expelled if she is caught cheating in this way. Colleges are a place for learning and thinking. They want their students to take their work seriously, take credit for their own hard work, but also to give credit to others. This is why when students write papers, they have to cite all their references. It is central to academic honesty. Students who break this rule risk losing their right to participate in the college's academic life. That is, students like Sofia can be expelled. If Sofia is expelled, not only will she lose her scholarship, but she might also jeopardize her chances of being accepted into another college. If the new school asks her why she decided to transfer, will she lie again and hide the fact that she was expelled? The new college may ask for letters of recommendation from the first school. Clearly, Sofia is putting her education and her future on the line.

In this example, the writer's first body paragraph follows the model for a persuasive essay that you studied in Unit 2. The topic sentence states a major reason why Sofia should not use the "A" paper: she may have trouble continuing her education if she gets caught. The rest of the sentences in the first paragraph provide supporting details about the reason.

In the next paragraph of the essay, the writer might choose to:

- provide or explain another reason why Sofia shouldn't use the paper (persuasive)

- describe the possible results this choice might have on Sofia's life (cause-effect)

- propose a solution to the problem other than using the paper (problem-solution)

To help you decide how to organize your body paragraphs, think about your thesis statement and ask yourself questions like the ones on the next page. Your answers may help you write topic sentences and organize your body paragraphs.

Read the thesis statement on a different topic. Notice how the different types of questions can help the writer decide how to organize the body paragraphs of the essay.

Example:

Thesis Statement: Even thought Nico risks failing, asking Maureen to help him cheat on Tuesday's chemistry exam would be a serious mistake.

Persuasion

Ask Yourself: What are the advantages of asking Maureen to help him cheat?

What are the disadvantages of asking Maureen to help him cheat?

Who would have an opposing point of view? What would it be?

Problem-Solution

Ask Yourself: What problems do people face when studying for exams or cheating?

What solution(s) do I support? What would critics say about this solution?

Cause-Effect

Ask Yourself: What makes people to want to cheat?

What caused Nico to consider cheating?

What will happen is he asks Maureen?

What effects might cheating have on his education, Maureen's education, or his friendship with Maureen?

Focused Practice

A. *For the following essay assignment and thesis statement, write questions that you might think about for each organizational structure. The first one is done for you.*

> Kam is a 22 year-old college graduate living in California, where he and his parents settled after emigrating from Hong Kong when Kam was just a boy. Kam is considering his options for the future. He would very much like to be a professional chef; however, his father wants him to use his undergraduate science degree and pursue a Ph.D. in physics. In your opinion, what is the best choice for Kam? To support your point of view, you may want to discuss the advantages and disadvantages, or the causes and/or effects, of certain choices. You may also want to present solution(s) to the problem.

Thesis Statement: Although Kam would really like to become a chef, he should follow his father's wishes and get a Ph.D. in physics instead.

1. Persuasion

Ask Yourself: _What are the advantages of going to cooking school?_

What are the advantages of following his father's wishes?

Who would have an opposing point of view? What would it be?

(continued)

2. Problem-Solution

Ask Yourself: _____

_____

_____

3. Cause-Effect

Ask Yourself: _____

_____

_____

B. *Choose two of the organizational structures from Exercise A. Answer the questions you wrote. Then write a topic sentence for a body paragraph based on your answer. Follow the example.*

Organizational Structure: *Persuasion*

Ask Yourself: *What are the advantages of going to cooking school?*

Possible Answer: *Kam will have a career that he enjoys.*

Ask Yourself: *What are the advantages of following his father's wishes?*

Possible Answer: *He will be showing his father respect, and he won't have to listen to his father's criticism.*

Ask Yourself: *Who would have an opposing point of view? What would it be?*

Possible Answer: *His sisters or brothers might think that Kam should follow his dreams because he lives in a new culture and there are new rules. In this country young people make their own choices,*

Possible Topic Sentence: *One reason that Kam should follow his father's wishes is that it will make his relationship with his father more positive.*

Organizational Structure: _____

Ask Yourself: _____

    Possible Answer: _____

                       _____

                       _____

Ask Yourself: _____

    Possible Answer: _____

                       _____

                       _____

Possible Topic Sentence: _____

                       _____

Organizational Structure: _____

Ask Yourself: _____

    Possible Answer: _____

                       _____

                       _____

Ask Yourself: _____

    Possible Answer: _____

                       _____

                       _____

Possible Topic Sentence: _____

                       _____

Signaling Paragraph Organization

When using multiple organizational structures, writers often use words and phrases that tell the reader which structures are being used in the paragraph. This helps the reader follow the writer's reasoning to see how the paragraph supports the thesis statement.

The following words and phrases help your reader understand the organizational structure of your body paragraph.

Persuasion	Problem-Solution	Cause-Effect
advantages/disadvantages benefits/drawbacks	problem, issue, dilemma solve, solution	affect cause effect, result, consequence because, since therefore, as a consequence as a result of, because of

In the following example, the writer uses *will result, consequences, affected, as a result, as a consequence*, and *therefore*. These words and expressions all signal a cause-effect structure.

Example:

Thesis Statement: I believe that the risks outweigh the benefits in this situation. It would be foolish for Sofia to use the online paper.

> If she thinks about it carefully, Sofia will realize that choosing to use the paper from the Internet will result in tremendous risks. Being caught would have terrible consequences. Sofia risks being expelled from the college, and as a result, her future would be seriously affected. Because of her academic record at this college, she risks never being able to get into another college and fulfilling her dream of becoming a nurse. Further, she risks losing the respect of her professor and her classmates. She will have to face the embarrassment of being caught by her professor, and her classmates will likely realize that her actions could have lowered their grades because the professor used the bell curve. As a consequence, they will resent her for trying to take the easy way out while they worked hard. Everyone knows that Sofia has struggled all semester. Therefore, they will certainly be suspicious if she gets one of the highest grades in the class on the final paper. There would be no sympathy for Sofia if she got caught.

Focused Practice

In the following body paragraphs, underline the parts that signal the organizational structure. Write the name of the structure on the line below each paragraph.

1.

> First, there are both advantages and disadvantages that come with the decision to use the Internet paper. In the best-case scenario, Sofia will use the plagiarized paper and receive an "A." She'll pass the course and continue on with her education and her life. However, Sofia must also consider the worst-case scenario. What are the chances that she will get caught? I think they're pretty high. Most professors can tell whether a student has written a paper or whether the paper comes from another source. In a class of 20–25 students, the professor might be familiar with Sofia's writing and recognize the writing as not being hers. If it is a big lecture hall, then there is no problem. There is also a chance, though, that the professor might recognize the paper itself. The professor may have given this assignment to another group of students, so Sofia may not be the first student to have used the paper. If the professor discovers that the paper was plagiarized, Sofia will be expelled from college. To me, the benefits just aren't worth the risks.

Organizational structure: _____

2.

> Furthermore, with a little more effort, Sofia might see another solution to her dilemma. That is, if she works harder, she might actually pass the course and solve her problem. From the case, we do not know if Sofia has used the college's resources to help students who are having difficulty. There may be tutors in the economics department available to help her. She could join a study group of students in her class. She could also go to see her professor during office hours and talk through some of the material in the course that she finds difficult. The professor may also offer her an extra credit assignment that may boost her grade. Ultimately, there may be a way for Sofia to pass the course and resolve the issue. Will this extra help come too late? Frankly, it could; however, the lesson for Sofia will be to get help as soon as she begins having trouble in her classes and not wait until the last minute. Then again, she might surprise herself.

Organizational structure: _____

Your Own Writing

Planning Your Body Paragraphs

A. *Review your thesis statement and think about these questions.*

1. Which ideas in my thesis statement need to be explained or supported in the essay?

_____

2. How many body paragraphs will I need to support my thesis? _____

What organizational structure would be best for each body paragraph?

_____

_____

B. *Before you begin writing your body paragraphs, complete the following outline. Copy your thesis statement from page 167.*

- Complete the outline for your body paragraphs. Be sure to include at least two organizational structures.

Essay with Multiple Organizational Structures

▶ Thesis Statement: _____

_____

    ▶ Body Paragraph 1

        ▶ Organizational Structure: _____

        ▶ Topic Sentence 1: _____

        _____

        ▶ Development and Support:

        _____

        _____

        _____

        _____

▶ Body Paragraph 2

    ▶ Organizational Structure: _____

    ▶ Topic Sentence 2: _____

        _____

    ▶ Development and Support:

        _____

        _____

        _____

        _____

▶ Body Paragraph 3 (Optional)

    ▶ Organizational Structure: _____

    ▶ Topic Sentence 3: _____

        _____

    ▶ Development and Support:

        _____

        _____

        _____

        _____

C. Checking in. *Share your outline with a partner. Did your partner . . .*

- use at least two organizational structures?
- write topic sentences that are appropriate for the organizational structures?
- provide interesting supporting details?

D. *Based on your partner's feedback, you may want to rewrite parts of your outline.*

■ THE CONCLUSION

As you know, a concluding paragraph has two key parts:

- a sentence that restates the thesis statement
- a concluding strategy that helps wrap up the essay

In an essay with multiple organizational structures, one effective concluding strategy is to return to the opening strategy you used in the introduction. You can:

1. Answer or make a comment about the question you posed.

2. Complete the story you started with.

3. Comment on or add to the interesting fact that you mentioned.

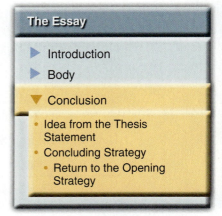

You might also combine the previous concluding strategy with others you have learned in previous units:

- Look to the future.
- Propose a solution to the problem.
- Comment on the significance of your analysis.

Focused Practice

Read the following thesis statement and concluding paragraph. Answer the questions. Then discuss your answers with a partner.

Thesis Statement: I believe that the risks outweigh the benefits in this situation. It would be foolish for Sofia to use the online paper.

> In conclusion, plagiarizing a paper to pass a course is simply not worth the risk. Clearly, this is a tough choice because there is so much at stake, but using the paper is not a wise choice. The risk is simply too great. In addition, I think Sofia is trying to take the easy way out—the choice that will be easiest for her with little consideration for the effect her choice would have on others. Sofia's easy way out carries a risk for her classmates. Because the professor grades on a bell curve, Sofia's choice could affect other students' grades and their overall academic records. As the prisoner's dilemma suggests, it is usually a mistake to betray—to choose the option that does not benefit the group. I believe that the best solution is for Sofia to write the best paper she can and then face the consequences—good or bad—like a mature adult. This is the only ethical choice.

1. What is the writer's restated thesis? Circle the sentence or sentences.

2. What concluding strategy or strategies does the writer use? _____

_____

Your Own Writing

Planning Your Conclusion

A. *How will you rephrase your thesis statement in the conclusion? List your ideas here.*

_____

_____

_____

B. *In addition to returning to the opening strategy, what other strategy or strategies will you use to close the essay?*

_____

_____

_____

C. Checking in. *Share your ideas with a partner. Did your partner . . .*

- discover a new and interesting way to rephrase the thesis statement?

- return to the opening strategy?

- use an additional concluding strategy?

Writing Your First Draft

A. *Review your notes on pages 162, 167, and 174–175. Then write the first draft of your essay. When you are finished, give your essay a working title. Hand in your draft to your teacher.*

> **Tip for Writers**
>
> **Check that** the basic **purpose** of your essay **is clear and** that the **organizational structures** you chose for your body paragraphs **support your thesis statement and help accomplish your purpose.**

Revising your work is an essential part of the writing process. This is your opportunity to be sure that your essay has all of the important pieces and that it is clear.

Focused Practice

A. *You have read parts of this essay already. Now read the entire essay to see how the parts fit together.*

Sofia's Choice

What would you risk for a passing grade in one of your courses? Sofia Simons is a college student struggling to pass her economics class. Because she did poorly on the midterm exam, she needs to get an "A" on her final paper in order to pass the course and keep the scholarship that allows her to pay for her classes. Interestingly, she may have a possible solution to her problem. Sofia discovered an economics paper on a website that offers student papers for a fee. The paper she found was rated as excellent, and it covers the same topic that Sofia's professor assigned. At the moment, she is debating whether or not to use this paper. It would mean plagiarizing, but Sofia may want to take that risk in order to pass the course. I believe that the risks outweigh the benefits in this situation. It would be foolish for Sofia to use the online paper.

First, there are both benefits and drawbacks that come with the decision to use the Internet paper. In the best-case scenario, Sofia will use the paper she found on the Internet, receive an "A," pass the course, and continue with her education. She will have plagiarized, but she wouldn't be caught. Her long-term benefit would be getting her degree while maintaining her scholarship. She could pursue her dream of having a nursing career. However, the chances of being caught are high. Most professors can tell whether a student has written a paper or whether the paper comes from another source. In a small class of 20–25 students, the professor might be familiar with Sofia's writing style and recognize the Internet paper as not being hers. If it is a big lecture class, this might not be a problem. There is, however, a chance that the professor might recognize the paper itself. The professor may have given this assignment to another group of students, and Sofia may not be the first student to have used the paper. In the worst-case scenario, the drawbacks are serious and clear. The professor will discover that Sofia's paper was plagiarized and act according to the school's academic honesty policy. If Sofia were expelled, she

(continued)

---

might never be able to get into another college with expulsion on her academic record. Ultimately, her dream of becoming a nurse would be destroyed.

On the other hand, if Sofia chooses not to use the "A" paper from the Internet, she is left with the original problem. She will most likely fail the course and probably lose her scholarship. One solution would be to take a leave of absence from school until she has enough money to return, and this might not be such a no-win situation. Leaving school could actually work in her favor. True, it is not what she had planned, but taking a new direction, at least for a few months or a year, could be a reasonable and acceptable solution. She is a nursing major. She could probably get some practical experience in that area and gain important insights about her chosen career. She would also have made an admirable and ethical choice. In reality, this dilemma could be an opportunity for her.

Furthermore, there are a number of actions she could take that could drastically affect the outcome of this situation. Because Sofia is a full-time student, there are most likely many resources at the college that help students who are having difficulty. There may be tutors in the economics department available to help her. She could join a study group of students in her class. She could also go see her professor during office hours and talk through some of the material in the course that she finds difficult. The professor may also offer her an extra credit assignment that could boost her grade. Exploring and using these types of resources might not only increase Sofia's chances of success in the course, but also boost her confidence. As a result, Sofia might actually pass the course.

In the end, Sofia has to decide what she is willing to risk for a passing grade in this course. Clearly, this is a tough choice for her because there is so much at stake, but I believe that using the paper would be a terrible mistake. In addition, I think Sofia is trying to take the easy way out—the choice that will be easiest for her with little consideration for the effect her choice would have on others. Sofia's easy way out carries a risk for her classmates. Because the professor grades on a bell curve, Sofia's choice could affect other students' grades and their overall academic records. As the prisoner's dilemma suggests, it is usually a mistake to betray—to choose the option that does not benefit the group. Sofia should try to write the best paper she can and then face the consequences—good and bad—like a mature adult. This is the only ethical choice.

B. *Work with a partner. Answer the questions about the essay.*

1. In the introduction, which type of opening strategy did the writer use to attract the readers' attention? _____

2. What is the thesis statement? Underline the thesis statement sentence(s).

3. What is the controlling idea of paragraph 2? Underline the sentence that states it.

4. What is the organizational structure of paragraph 2? _____

5. What transition words or expressions does the writer use to connect ideas between paragraphs? Circle them.

6. What is the controlling idea of paragraph 3? Underline the sentence that states it.

7. What is the organizational structure of paragraph 3? _____

8. What is the controlling idea of paragraph 4? Underline the sentence that states it.

9. What is the organizational structure of paragraph 4? _____

10. In the conclusion, how does the writer return to the opening strategy?

    _____

11. What other concluding strategy does the writer use?

    _____

C. **Checking in.** *Discuss your marked-up essay with another pair of students. Then in your group, share one thing about the essay that you found the most interesting. Explain your answer.*

Building Word Knowledge

Using Idioms. The writer used several idioms in "Sofia's Choice" including the ones below.

take the easy way out: to end a difficult situation in a way that seems easy but is not the best or smartest way

the best-case (or worst-case) scenario: the best (or the worst) possible situation or result

work in (someone's) favor: to be beneficial to a person or group

no-win situation: a situation in which there is a problem with no satisfactory solution

Notice how these idioms are used in "Sofia's Choice" on page 178. Then review Building Word Knowledge on pages 157 and 180. Complete each sentence with an appropriate idiom from the box. Use each idiom only once.

be at stake	take the easy way out
best-case scenario	win-win situation
no-win situation	work in (someone's) favor
sleep on it	worst-case scenario

1. **Bob:** I *hate* going to weddings! I don't want to go. Can't I just send a nice gift instead?

   Ray: I understand, but in this situation you can't _____. Go

   to the wedding!

2. **Alice:** Any suggestions for my job interview tomorrow?

   Flo: It will _____ if you express interest in the company and

   show how you can contribute to its success.

3. **Andrew:** I can see that you have a really tough choice. Any decision you make will

   have a negative impact.

   James: That's what makes it so difficult. I'm going to _____

   and give them my final decision tomorrow, but I think it's just a

   _____.

4. **Bill:** How is our business doing this year?

   Melinda: Terrible! We need to increase our sales. We aren't making any profits. The

   company's survival _____.

5. **Steve:** One of us is going to win! If I have the winning ticket, I will share the prize

   with you.

   Adam: OK, and if *I* have the winning ticket, I will share my prize with you. A

   _____!

6. **Gabriella:** Congratulations! You made it to the final round of the chess competition.

   Esther: Thanks! I hope I win!

   Gabriella: In the _____ you will come in first place, and in

   the _____ you will come in second in the world.

   That's not too bad either.

Your Own Writing

Revising Your Draft

A. Reread the first draft of your essay. Use the Revision Checklist to identify parts of your writing that might need improvement.

B. Review your plans and notes and your responses to the Revision Checklist. Then revise your first draft. Save your revised essay. You will look at it again in the next section.

Revision Checklist

Did you . . .

☐ organize the body paragraphs in your essay in a way that best supports your purpose?

☐ use an opening strategy to attract the readers' interest?

☐ give enough background information in your introduction?

☐ present the controlling idea of the essay in a clear thesis statement?

☐ use effective topic sentences?

☐ use transition and signal words and phrases?

☐ return to the controlling idea in the thesis statement in your conclusion?

☐ return to the opening strategy in the concluding paragraph?

☐ use an additional concluding strategy?

☐ give your essay an interesting title?

☐ use idioms correctly?

GRAMMAR PRESENTATION

Before you hand in your revised essay, you must check it for any errors in grammar, punctuation, and spelling. In this section you will learn about real and unreal conditionals. You will focus on this grammar when you edit and proofread your essay.

Real and Unreal Conditionals: Present and Future

Grammar Notes	Examples
Present Real Conditionals	
1. Use **present real conditional** sentences for **general truths**. The **if clause** talks about the **condition**, and the **result clause** talks about **what happens** if the condition occurs. Use the **present** in both clauses.	*if* clause result clause • **If** the players **think** carefully, they **see** that they can reduce their overall risk by cooperating. *if* clause • **If** prisoners **give** evidence against each other, result clause they **are defecting**.
USAGE NOTE: We often use **even if** when the **result is surprising**.	*if* clause result clause • **Even if** we are lucky, we sometimes **face** a no-win situation.
2. You can use **modals** (*can, should, might, must . . .*) in the **result clause**.	modal • **If** Sofia **thinks about it**, she **can make** an ethical choice,
3. A **conditional sentence** does not always have **if**. You can often use **when** instead of **if**. This is especially true when you talk about general truths, habits, and things that happen again and again.	• **When** the prisoners **give** evidence against each other, they **are defecting**. • **When** people **play** the game repeatedly, they **cooperate** more often. *(continued)*

Future Real Conditionals

1. Use **future real conditional** sentences to talk about what **will happen under certain conditions**.

The *if clause* gives the **condition**. The **result clause** gives the **probable** or **certain result**. Use the **simple present** in the *if clause*. Use the **future** with *will* or *be going to* in the **result clause**.

BE CAREFUL! Even though the *if clause* refers to the future, use the **simple present**.

if clause   result clause
• *If* you both **confess**, you **will** each **go** to prison.

simple present   future
• *If* you both **confess**, you **will** each **go** to prison.

simple present   future
• *If* you both **confess**, you **are** each **going to go** to prison.

• *If* one prisoner **confesses**, he **will go** free.
NOT: If one prisoner ~~will confess,~~ he **will go** free.

2. You can also use **modals** (*can, should, might, must . . .*) in the **result clause**.

USAGE NOTE: We sometimes use *then* to *emphasize the result* in future real conditionals with **modals** or *will*.

• If Sofia gets a good grade on the essay, she
   modal
 might **pass** the course.

• If Sofia gets a good grade on the essay, *then* she *might* **pass** the course.

Present and Future Unreal Conditionals

1. Use **present and future unreal conditional** sentences to talk about **unreal conditions and their results**. A condition and its result may be untrue, imagined, or impossible.

The *if clause* gives the **unreal condition**, and the **result clause** gives the **unreal result** of that condition.

The sentence can be about
• the present
  OR
• the future

    if clause
• *If* people **cooperated** more often, the world
  result clause
 would be a better place.
(*But people don't cooperate, so the world isn't a good place.*)

    if clause
• *If* people **cooperated** more often these days,
  result clause
 the world **would be** a better place.

   if clause   result clause
• *If* Sofia *left school* next semester, she *would work* full-time.
(*But she's not going to leave school next semester, so she won't work full-time.*)

2. Use the **simple past** in the *if clause*.

Use *would* + **base form** of the verb in the **result clause**.

BE CAREFUL! The *if* clause uses the simple past, but the **meaning is NOT past**.

Do **NOT use would** in the *if clause*.

Use *were* for **all subjects** when the verb in the *if clause* is a form of *be*.

USAGE NOTE: Some people use *was* with *I*, *he*, *she*, and *it*. However this is usually considered incorrect, especially in formal or written English.

simple past	would + base form

- *If* she **had** a better grade, Sofia **wouldn't be** so worried about the paper.

- *If* she **had** a better grade now, Sofia **wouldn't be** so worried about the paper.

- *If* she **knew** she had a chance to pass, she **would write** her own paper.
NOT: **If** she ~~would know~~ she had a chance . . .

- *If* Sofia **were** an *A* student, she **would have** no worries.
NOT: **If** Sofia ~~was~~ an *A* student . . .

3. You can also use *might* or *could* in the **result clause**, but the meaning is different from *would*.

a. Use *would* if the result is **certain**. Do NOT use *will* in unreal condtional sentences.

b. Use *might* or *could* if the result is **not certain**. Do NOT use *may* or *can*.

- If Sofia got an "A" on the essay, she *would* **pass** the course.
NOT: If Sofia got an "a", she ~~will~~ pass the course.

- If Sofia studied harder, she *might* **pass** the course.
NOT: If Sofia studied harder, she ~~may~~ pass the course.

OR

- If Sofia studied harder, she *could* **pass** the course.
NOT: If Sofia studied harder, she ~~can~~ pass the course.

4. You can begin conditional sentences with the *if clause* or the **result clause**. The meaning is the same.

BE CAREFUL! Use a **comma** between the two clauses only when the *if clause comes first*.

- You **will** each **spend** 6 months in prison *if* you both **stay** silent.

- *If* you both **stay** silent, you **will** each **spend** six months in prison.

Focused Practice

A. *Review the dilemma on page 155. Then complete the sentences with the correct form of the verbs given.*

Real Conditionals

1. If Country A _____ Planet X first, Country B _____
   (reach)   (not / be able to)
   control the natural resources there.

2. Country A _____ Country B to share the natural resources if Country B
   (ask)

   _____ on Planet X first.
   (land)

3. If Country A _____ to explore Planet X, there _____ less
   (try)   (be)
   money to spend on jobs, health care, and education.

4. If either country _____ a lot of money on space exploration, the
   (spend)

   citizens _____ very upset.
   (be)

5. If politicians _____ why they want to go to Planet X, citizens
   (explain)

   _____ their minds about the idea.
   (change)

Unreal Conditionals

1. Countries _____ interested in going to Planet X if it
   (not / be)

   _____ useful natural resources.
   (not / have)

2. It _____ possible for humans to get there if Planet X
   (not / be)

   _____ so close to Earth,
   (not / be)

3. If country A _____ Planet X, it
   (control)

   _____ much more power than other countries.
   (have)

4. If any nation _____ weapons on Planet X, other countries
   (put)

   _____ in danger.
   (be)

5. If I _____ the president of Country A, I
   (be)

   _____.

B. *Read and edit the sentences. There are eight errors in the use of conditionals. Some sentences may have more than one error. The first error has already been corrected. Find and correct seven more.*

1. If Sofia copies the "A" paper, there ~~are~~ *will be* fewer A's for other students in the class.

2. Sofia will fail, if she doesn't get an "A."

3. I think Sofia just doesn't study hard enough. She will get better grades if she studied harder.

4. If Sofia did not get an "A" on the paper, she will lose her scholarship.

5. If she was more responsible, she would ask for extra help instead of cheating.

6. If Sofia plagiarized the paper the professor will notice that she cheated.

7. If the other students in her class find out that she plagiarized, they would be upset.

C. *Write five sentences related to the assignment you chose on page 160 or 161. Use conditionals. These may be sentences you already have in your essay.*

1. _____

2. _____

3. _____

4. _____

5. _____

Your Own Writing

Editing Your Draft

A. *Use the Editing Checklist to edit and proofread your essay.*

B. *Prepare a clean copy of the final draft of your essay and hand it in to your teacher.*

Editing Checklist

Did you . . .

☐ include real or unreal conditionals and use them correctly?

☐ use correct verb forms, punctuation, and spelling?

☐ include idioms and use them correctly?

Appendix

■ RESEARCHING A TOPIC

Use the library and the Internet to find out more about your topic. For each source you use, record the author, title, date, publisher, and medium (e.g., print, Web, DVD).

Using Resources. The library contains a wide range of printed books, magazines, and reference materials (encyclopedias, atlases, and books of facts) that you can use to find information. Look for two or three books or articles with information about your topic. Although you can begin researching your topic in an encyclopedia, most instructors will not allow you to use this information as a cited source in your paragraph or essay. If you find information in an encyclopedia, look at the end of the entry for titles of individual books and articles about your topic; try to locate and use these sources.

One of the quickest ways to search for information is to use the Internet. Today, many books, articles, and reference books are available online. To do an online search, select keywords or a key question. Then type it into a search engine, such as Google, Yahoo, or Bing. Keep your online search as narrow as possible. Otherwise you will have to look through too many sources.

Suppose that you wanted to find out about the legally blind musher Rachael Scdoris who competed in the Iditarod in 2005. Here are some examples of specific keywords and questions that would help you find sources about her.

Examples:

Keywords:
Iditarod competitor Rachael Scdoris
Rachael Scdoris and the 2005 Iditarod

Key Questions:
Who is the Iditarod competitor Rachael Scdoris?
What happened when Rachael Scdoris competed in the 2005 Iditarod?

Evaluating Resources. Once you locate a source, think critically about it.

- When was it published? Is it up-to-date?
- Is it published by a well-known and reliable place (e.g., a mainstream newspaper or government website)?
- Does it present a balanced and unbiased point of view, or is it only expressing one person's opinion?
- Does it contain facts that can be double-checked in another source?

Evaluate each source you use, especially the sources you find on the Internet. Some Internet sites contain inaccurate information, so limit your sources to trusted sites.

■ CITING SOURCES IN YOUR WRITING

When you are writing a paragraph or essay, always acknowledge your sources of information or any wording that is not your own. If you do not cite your sources, including the words, ideas, or research that you have borrowed from others, you are *plagiarizing*, or stealing other people's ideas. This is a serious offense that is treated very severely in an academic environment.

In colleges and universities, one of the most commonly used styles for handling citations is the MLA (Modern Language Association) style. According to the MLA style, you cite your sources in two places: within the text and in a "Works Cited" list.*

In-Text Citations. Most of the wording in your paragraphs and essays should be your own. When you paraphrase or quote what other people have said or researched, give a brief citation for the source in parentheses at the end of the sentence. If you have already mentioned the author within the sentence, you do not need to repeat the name at the end.

Examples:

Citing a Fact: According to a 2011 report, Twitter has only 21 million active users (Bennett).

Citing a Paraphrase: The legendary journalist spoke of the need to support public broadcasting (Moyers). [or] Bill Moyers, a legendary journalist, spoke of the need to support public broadcasting.

Citing a Quote: On her website, the legally blind musher says: "I hope my story can help encourage others to pursue their dreams" (Scdoris).

A List of Works Cited. At the end of your writing, provide a list of all the sources you have cited. Type "Works Cited" at the top of the list and center the heading. Then organize your sources alphabetically according to the author's last name. If the source has no author, alphabetize it according to its title. Indent the second line of the source.

The basic format for individual citations and a "Works Cited" list is shown in the examples below.

Examples:

For Articles: Author. "Article Title." *Magazine Title* date: page no. medium.

For Books: Author. *Book Title*. publisher, date: page no. medium.

For Personal Interviews: Name of Interviewee. Personal interview. date.

For Websites: Website title. publisher, date. medium. date accessed. <URL>

Works Cited

Collum, Danny Duncan. "How to save journalism: can a government-subsidized press save democracy?" *Sojourners* June 2009: 40. Print.

Miller, Claire Cain. "The New News Junkie Is Online and On the Phone." *New York Times* 1 Mar. 2010. Print.

Noone, Joan. Personal interview. 20 July 2011.

---

* The format for citing other sources can also be found in MLA handbooks, on the websites for most college and university libraries in North America, or by searching the Internet using the keywords *MLA style*. For electronic sources, MLA style no longer requires writers to include Web addresses, or URLs, but some instructors may still require them. Some instructors will also allow you to use citation generators that are available online. Check with your teacher about his or her requirements.

Index

Acknowledgments

I would like to extend deep appreciation and thanks to the students and faculty in the Department of Developmental Skills/ESL at Borough of Manhattan Community College, City University of New York, for their insights and support. Thanks in particular to colleagues and friends Sarah Nakamaru and Sharon Avni for their feedback on drafts of this work. Also, my sincere thanks to Debbie Sistino, Joan Poole, my wonderful editor Nan Clarke, and the staff at Pearson, for their talent and tireless dedication to this project.

John Beaumont

Credits